SATANISM

Satanism

Is It Real?

Father Jeffrey J. Steffon

Servant Publications
Ann Arbor, Michigan

Scripture texts used in this work, unless otherwise indicated, are taken
from *The Revised Standard Version* of the Bible, copyright © 1946, 1952,
and 1971, by the Division of Christian Education of the National
Council of Churches of Christ in the U.S.A., and are used by permission.

Published by Servant Publications
P.O. Box 8617
Ann Arbor, Michigan 48107

The names and characterizations in this book drawn from the authors's
case studies or his personal experience are rendered pseudonymously and
as fictional composites. Any similarity between the names and characterizations of these individuals and real people is unintended and purely
coincidental.

Cover design by Michael Andaloro
Cover art from Scala/Art Resource, New York

 93 94 95 96 10 9 8 7 6 5 4 3 2
Printed in the United States of America

ISBN 0-89283-777-2

Nihil obstat: Monsignor Joseph Pollard, STD
            Censor Deputatus

Imprimatur: Cardinal Roger Mahony, D.D.
            Archbishop of Los Angeles
            November 14, 1991

The *Nihil Obstat* and *Imprimatur* are official declarations that the work
contains nothing contrary to Faith and Morals. It is not implied
thereby that those granting the *Nihil Obstat* and *Imprimatur* agree with
the contents, statements, or opinions expressed.

Library of Congress Cataloging-in-Publication Data

Steffon, Jeffrey J., 1954– .
    Satanism : is it real? / Jeffrey J. Steffon.
        p. cm.
    Includes bibliographical references
    ISBN 0-89283-777-2
    1. Devil. 2. Satanism. 3. Occultism. 4. Catholic Church—
    Doctrines. I. Title.
    BT981.S73   1992
    235'.4—dc20   92-3590

Dedication

To my niece Julia,
who died of cancer at the age of fifteen.
May her soul,
and all the souls of the faithful departed,
through the mercy of God
rest in peace. Amen.

Contents

Acknowledgments / 9
Prayer to St. Michael / 10
Introduction / 11

Part One: Who Is Satan?
1. Satan in the Bible and Catholic Tradition / 25
    Satan Is a Fallen Angel Opposed to God / 28
    The Church's Abiding Belief / 31
    Conclusion / 33
2. Satan: His Nature and Activity among Us / 35
    The Battle Is Daily / 37
    A Story of God's Protection / 40

Part Two: Satan's Deceptions
3. Lie Number One: Divination / 43
    The Ouija Board / 43
    The Tarot / 45
    Palmistry / 46
    Rod and Pendulum / 47
    Astrology / 47
    Necromancy / 50
    Divination and the Bible / 52
4. Transcendental Meditation / 57
    Meditation that Is Christian / 61
5. Witchcraft / 65
    Dungeons and Dragons / 68
6. Sorcery / 73
    Drugs and Objects in Satanism or Sorcery / 75
    Symbols of Evil / 77
    Santeria / 80
    Saints versus Orishas / 85
7. New Age and Neo-Pagan Movements / 91
    Reincarnation: Saving Oneself / 95

    Crystals, Colors, Channeling, and Past-Life Recall / 98
    Wicca: Goddess Worship / 102
    Cabala: Twisting Scripture / 103
    The Enneagram: Offshoot of Islam / 105
  8. Satanism / 111
    The Magick of Aleister Crowley / 114
    Anton LaVey: An American Crowley / 117
    Levels of Satanism / 119
    Covens in the United States / 122
    Ritual Abuse: A Legal Problem / 125
    The Lure of Satanic Cults / 128
    Satanic Ritual Child Abuse / 132
    Symptoms of Ritual Abuse / 136
    The Black Mass / 143
    Satanic Ritual Calendar / 144

Part Three: Freedom from Darkness
  9. Renouncing the Occult / 147
    The Armor of Prayer and Faith / 150
    Chaplet of St. Michael the Archangel / 156
    Chaplet of the Holy Spirit / 158
    Chaplet of the Sacred Heart / 159
    Chaplet of the Divine Mercy / 160
    Helping Teens Stay out of Satanism / 161
 10. Diabolical Possession and Deliverance / 167
    Determining Diabolical Possession / 168
    Characteristics of the Possessed / 170
    Means of Deliverance / 174
    Stories of Deliverance / 177
    Conclusion / 180

Appendix One: Scripture References on Satan / 181
*Appendix Two: Church Pronouncements and Writings of Early
    Church Fathers on Satan* / 187
Notes / 193
Glossary / 203
Bibliography / 209

ACKNOWLEDGMENTS

FIRST, I WOULD LIKE TO THANK MY PARENTS, Joseph and Julia Steffon, because they fostered my vocation to the priesthood. I thank Cardinal Timothy Manning for ordaining me a priest. I thank St. Joseph Parish Prayer Group, Pomona, California, through whom I learned about the charismatic renewal. I thank Anne Petteruto, Fr. Richard Woldum, and Fr. Michael Burns for their input and support in writing this book. I thank the members of Our Lady of Peace Prayer Group, Sepulveda, California, for their prayers during this past year. I thank Rachel Ortega-Gonzales for proofreading the text. And I thank the Catholic priests and Protestant ministers, who pioneered study in the field of the occult. "May the favor of the Lord Jesus Christ be with your spirit. Amen."

Prayer Invoking the Protection of St. Michael

Saint Michael, The Archangel,
defend us in the battle.
Be our protection against the wickedness
and snares of the devil.
May God rebuke him, we humbly pray,
and do thou, O Prince of the Heavenly Host,
by the power of God, thrust into hell
Satan and all evil spirits
who wander through the world
for the ruin of souls.
Amen.

Introduction

Is SATAN REAL? Consider the following situation which seemed understandable enough at first. Theresa obtained my name from one of her friends. She was in counseling, in addition to meeting with her parish priest every other week. She wanted to talk to me because she had viewed a video tape of a talk I had given on spiritual warfare.

Theresa was in her forties and had just gone through a divorce about two years earlier. In working through her divorce, other issues started to surface. At first, this seemed natural enough. But then she began to remember some experiences in her childhood that were extremely painful. One day she showed some pictures and writing she had done to her parish priest. He told her that she should ask her counselor's impression about this material. Her counselor, a woman, was evasive in her answer. The following week Theresa again asked her priest what he thought about the pictures. He told her that the pictures described abuse—a particularly evil kind of abuse.

The following week she reported to her counselor what her priest had said. The counselor told her that she believed the latest pictures and writings indicated that she had been the victim of satanic ritual child abuse, confirming her priest's concern. Knowing from her friends that I counseled and prayed with such people, Theresa sought me out. I vividly remember our first meeting.

Theresa showed me some of her artwork. She also showed me writing that she had done over the past couple of months.

11

All the material indicated such abuse had indeed occurred. We talked about her reasons for wanting an appointment with me. We talked about her childhood and the things going on in her sessions with her counselor and her parish priest. She shared with me that she had "her children" with her and they needed help. "Her children" were different personalities. Theresa suffered from a multiple-personality disorder, which is not uncommon for victims of satanic ritual abuse. I asked her about "her children." She described ten different persons that talked within her.

At that point, I felt it would be good to pray and ask Jesus what he wanted me to do. I asked her to close her eyes and place herself in the presence of Jesus. Suddenly, she started to cry. She spoke with the voice of a child, saying, "Get that out of my mouth! I don't want that in my mouth. I want my mommy! Get away from me. Take that out of my mouth. I don't want to swallow. Take it out of my mouth." She was crying during this part of our session.

I invited Jesus to walk into this painful moment of her life. He was able to comfort the hurt little girl within. She gradually stopped crying, experiencing peace in Jesus' loving arms. We then ended our session and set up a schedule for her to come in and receive prayer for inner healing. There is much that still needs to be healed in her. As of today three of her separate personalities have been integrated into her core personality. I believe that through the power of the love of Jesus her separate personalities will be fully integrated into her core personality some day.

Later on the day of our first session, as I was praying, I asked, "How could people be so cruel as to abuse a child in that manner?" I had read that in satanic ritual abuse the perpetrators force children to eat feces. Some of them force the children to have sexual relations with them. How dare they do this to God's little ones! I really felt outraged at the perpetrators. I was determined to do all that I could to help Theresa be healed of the horrors she had experienced as a vulnerable little girl.

Sadly, Theresa's story is not an isolated incident. I recently worked with Jacqueline in Idaho. Jacqueline also was a victim of satanic ritual abuse, and she had thirty-five different personalities. I saw her after twenty-seven of the personalities had been integrated into her core personality. They were starting to integrate the final eight personalities, but ran into some problems. Her therapist asked me to help because the therapy was not progressing. Within a month after my visit, the therapist was able to integrate the final eight personalities.

Cases of possible satanic ritual abuse are being discovered across the country. Television talk show hosts have even presented discussion panels on satanic ritual abuse and satanism. Tragically, vulnerable small children not only fall prey to satanism, teenagers are also attracted to the occult. Sometimes teens become involved in satanic gangs, called Stoners. I know of one of these gangs which sacrifices small animals at periodic intervals.

A girl from this gang became pregnant. The gang members wanted to sacrifice the child after it was born. The girl ran away from the gang. The child was born and given up for adoption. When she returned to the gang, she lied to gang members, telling them that she had had a miscarriage.

In the first week of November, 1991, a young girl was beaten to death in a small town in Arizona. The perpetrators of this vicious deed were her own classmates. Her death was a sacrifice to Satan.

Can these vicious actions simply be the result of human nature gone bad? Or is there something else which drives the perpetrators of satanic ritual abuse? Is it simply a rebellion against the morals of society or family? Could that drive people to murder babies in a sacrifice or beat a person to death in a ritual?

I believe that these unspeakably evil actions can, in large part, be explained by a personal, supranatural, evil being—Satan. Human beings are indeed capable of evil actions, but there is something peculiar and monstrous about the above incidents. It is as if they are beyond the scope of purely human behavior. It is actions such as these—particularly vicious, senseless, and unexplainable actions—in which Satan plays a part.

Yet there is a debate in the Catholic church today. Some theologians and priests say that there is no personal devil. They believe that evil is simply a lack of human goodness in the world. Satan is seen as simply a personification of humanity's dark side. Humanity is solely responsible for all the moral evil in the world. Other priests and theologians readily admit that much evil can be attributed to humanity, but believe that not all evil in the world can be fully explained by human sin alone.

This debate might make it seem as if Catholics can legitimately disagree on the existence of a personal devil. Yet the Catholic church has consistently taught in every age that there is a personal evil being—Satan. This teaching may surprise many since Satan is seldom mentioned in most Catholic parishes today. It has its foundation in the Bible and writings of the early Church Fathers. The reality of Satan is taught as well in the documents of the Second Vatican Council and other church councils.

Why don't many Catholics, including priests and theologians, believe in a personal devil, in spite of the church's clear and consistent teaching? I believe that such disbelief is part of a wider crisis in which there has been a breakdown in not only belief, but in practice of the faith. For example, Catholics today frequently disregard the church's teachings on artificial birth control. In recent years, Frs. Charles Curran and Matthew Fox, dissident theologians, have been disciplined by church authorities for errant teachings. Yet they continue to speak out and enjoy wide followings. A growing number of Catholics in our country do not attend Mass each Sunday. The current shortage of priests is becoming more acute, leaving ever more parishes "priestless." The Catholic church is sailing through stormy waters.

But the Catholic church is not the only institution in society that is facing a crisis. Consider the crisis in government. Governmental leaders disobey the law of the land. Five senators are accused of illegal dealings in a savings and loan scandal. Congressmen are writing bad checks. Some congressmen are accused of immoral acts with prostitutes and teenagers. Others are known drug users.

Before he was confirmed by the United States Senate, Supreme Court Justice Clarence Thomas was accused of sexual misconduct before the glare of television cameras. During the hearings of the Senate Judiciary Committee in the fall of 1991, both he and his accuser, Professor Anita Hill, were maligned without the protections and safeguards of a thorough investigation and due process of law. The reason for the hearings was the illegal leak of classified information by one of the Senate Judiciary Committee members. The hearings were a fiasco. The leaders of our country have allowed corruption and serious abuses of power to filter into our government.

The reality is that we live in an immoral world. The current movies and TV shows tell this generation's story: if you think you like somebody, go ahead—have sexual relations. Just practice safe sex. You don't need to be committed. "If it feels good, do it!" Teen sex is even being protrayed on prime-time television in the 1990s. For example, eighteen-year-old Doogie Howser, M.D., lost his virginity on the premiere episode of his show in the fall of 1991. And his show airs on a prime-time slot on the ABC television network.

Magic Johnson, star guard of the Los Angeles Lakers, was diagnosed positive with the HIV virus. This virus will eventually give him AIDS. In his first news conference, Mr. Johnson stated that he hopes to promote safe sex. In his terms, safe sex meant using a condom. But *the only sure safe sex is abstinence, a point Magic Johnson conceded several days after his first news conference.* The reason why Magic Johnson got the AIDS virus was because he lived promiscuously, as do many other professional athletes. He had sexual relations with someone else who had the virus, and he can't even remember who the infected partner was! The problem with the widespread epidemic of AIDS is promiscuity. If people simply abstained from sexual intercourse until marriage, the spread of AIDS would be greatly diminished.

The genre of horror movies has been particularly gruesome. Who hasn't seen shocking commercials and advertisements for *Friday the Thirteenth* and its sequels, the *Nightmare on Elm Street* series, and *Halloween* movies? Many deal with the occult: *The Holy Blood, The Terror Within, Hell High, Dance of the Damned, Witches,* and *The Omen* series. Pornography is flourishing. Drugs are sold in every community. Violent gangs rule many streets.

Many families are experiencing problems. With a 65 percent divorce rate, this is the age of the broken home. Young people are looking for answers, searching for something to hold on to. Society has largely failed to meet their needs.

Adolescence is difficult enough with rapid, embarrassing physical changes, leading to self-consciousness. With corresponding intellectual growth, teenagers begin to challenge the belief systems of the older generation, including those of their parents. It is difficult for them to tell the difference between expressing an ideal and working toward it, so they become disenchanted and often rebellious. This leaves them particularly prey to the occult and satanism.

THE TEENAGER'S DILEMMA

A common question for the teenager is: who am I? Erik Erickson believes it stems from the young person's confusion between his or her identity and role. To form their identity, teenagers must renegotiate their relationships with their parents. Separating from them and establishing an individual identity is normal and healthy, but often painful. This "rebellion" stage can be a real battleground. The pain and lack of understanding can be so strong that the teen fights every belief of the parents. He or she looks to parents for answers and finds none. A look at society uncovers hypocrisy. A look at the church is equally disappointing. Where do teenagers turn?

Maybe to alcohol. Maybe to marijuana and other drugs. Maybe to sex. But none of these avenues solves their underlying problems. Many turn to their peers as well and become heavily involved in the youth culture. In some cases, this then leads to occult involvement through rock music, videos, games, and even drugs and sex.

For most teenagers, experience with the occult is fleeting, mainly a curiosity. Others are truly looking to the occult for answers. Still others are rebelling against God. For some, the occult becomes a compelling, controlling force, causing them to lose all moral and ethical values.

For example, troubled teenagers who feel rejected by their parents and the church may start drinking and experimenting with drugs. It may seem innocent enough to the teenagers, since "everyone's doing it." In fact, there may be little or no direct occult involvement at first. Then drug and sex orgy parties may follow, cementing the teenagers' relationship with members of a satanic group. The next step may be involvement in an actual satanic ritual and even initiation into the group.

Before they fully realize it, these vulnerable youths discover that they are members of a satanic group and enslaved not only to satanism, but to drugs, sex, and alcohol. Even more alarming, if they threaten to leave the group or expose it, their lives and the lives of their loved one are typically threatened.

Tragically, many parents think that their teenager would never get involved in a satanic group and so are not alert to signs of possible occult involvement. Parents, pastors, and youth ministers need to realize that the occult is a growing infuence today. It is fueled by popular philosophies such as Wicca, the New Age Movement, and various neo-pagan movements, which are shaking the foundations of our Western wordview and Christianity

A CALL FROM GOD

In 1989 while I was praying, I felt a call from God to write a book on movements which might lead a person into the occult. For two years while researching the occult, I "toyed" with writing a book on the subject from the Catholic perspective. One August afternoon, I felt a strong call, as if God were saying to me, "Now is the time to write to my people about the dangers of Satan. Do not be afraid to do so. They are ready to hear what you will tell them."

Though the thrust of my book is primarily Catholic, I believe other Christians can benefit from its information. The Catholic view of Satan and the occult is confirmed by Scriptures and Catholic church teachings. This is the only age in which the existence of Satan as a personal evil being has been questioned. The reality of Satan must be established before there can be any competent discussion on the occult.

AN OVERVIEW OF THIS BOOK

First, the reader should keep in mind that all proper names used in case histories are fictitious to protect the confidentiality of the individuals involved.

In the first chapter we begin by asking: Who is Satan? Is he merely a part of human imagination? Is he an angel? Is he for real? Can human psychology alone explain sinister evil? We examine the teaching tradition of the Catholic church regarding Satan. The second chapter deals with Satan's activity in the world. What does he do? What is his primary objective? Satan is the deceiver of the human race, a fallen angel who takes pleasure in leading people away from God. He is a malicious, wicked being who tries to lead us away through lies.

In chapter three, we will look at some of the lies of Satan. This is the area of occult knowledge. Satan entices us through divination. He tries to trick us through meditative techniques. Chapter four warns us to be careful in meditative prayer. In our prayer we are to seek union with God.

In chapters five and six, another lure of Satan is exposed— the lure of power. Satan entices us with occult power to change the events surrounding our lives. But Satan always has a price for anything that he offers us. What about Dungeons and Dragons? Is it a harmless game? Or is it something that can lead one into satanism? Chapter six explains Santeria and its dangers.

In chapter eight of this book, Fran tells the story of how she witnessed the sacrifice of her own child at a satanic ritual. That is Satan at his "best." We also look at the people responsible for today's satanism and consider the terrible crime of the satanic ritual abuse of children, a growing phenomenon in today's society.

Though the New Age Movement, Wicca (contemporary witchcraft), and neo-pagan movements are not properly part of the occult, they are covered in chapter seven because they are doorways into the occult. For example, channeling, a prominent part of the New Age Movement, is another word for a séance, and a channelor is the medium. The worship of the goddess in Wicca is a return to paganism. Transcendental Meditation is based on an Eastern religion with a Tantric Yoga view of the world, a view that embraces reincarnation and karma. All are contrary to biblical teaching.

The last two chapters detail how one can be free from satanic influences through repentance and building a life with Jesus Christ. Some issues explored in these chapters are: Is it possible in today's world to be possessed by an evil spirit? If so, what are the criteria? How can parents and counselors alike help teenagers steer clear of satanism? The last chapter concludes with an explanation of deliverance prayer and the Catholic church's teaching on how to use this prayer in spiritual warfare.

Further, I have provided an appendix of scriptural refer-

ences to Satan and another appendix of church pronouncements and writings of the early Church Fathers on Satan.
Especially while reading Part One, readers may find review-
ing these references and writings helpful. Finally, to assist the
reader in understanding elements of satanism and the occult, I've provided illustrations of common satanic symbols in
chapter six and a glossary of common terms at the back of
the book.

HOW TO USE THIS BOOK

My hope is that priests, ministers, counselors, and parents
will find this book helpful as a resource in understanding
and then combating satanism and the occult. Priests and
ministers could use this book as an aid in educating their
congregrations about the dangers and deceptions of the face
of satanism today. It also might prove useful in counseling situations and in helping pastoral staff discern whether young
people in the parish are being lured into satanism and the
occult.

I sincerely hope that counselors and others in the helping
professions will read this book with an openness to understanding the spiritual dimension in their care of human
beings. A human being is composed of a body, mind, and
spirit. Physicians deal with the body. Psychologists deal with
the mind. But who deals with the spirit? Only priests and
ministers? No, counselors who are centered on Jesus can
effectively deal with the mind and spirit, getting at root spiritual causes in cases of satanic activity. The moving story of
Vicki in the last part of this book demonstrates this.

I hope that parents make use of this book as a guide. The
parents of teenagers are strategically placed to combat
satanism and the occult, but this book also provides clues for
discerning satanic activity at an earlier age. As the church
teaches, parents are the primary educators of their children
in the faith. They must know the lies and deceptions of Satan

and the occult if they are to counter satanism and form their children in the ways of Jesus Christ.

I pray that all who read this book may become aware of the ways that Satan entices them. I pray that those who read this book will put into practice the prayers contained in the last part. Prayer is the most effective means of combating the evil one. We are created by God to give him honor and glory. We have been redeemed by Jesus Christ, receiving the free gift of eternal life. We are being sanctified (being made holy) through the Holy Spirit.

In spite of the evil in our world, we can be supremely confident that Jesus is victorious over sin, death, and the evil one. By calling upon him and remaining grounded in him, we too can be victorious in exposing and combating the works of Satan. That is reason to glorify God and thank him for the victory he gives us in Jesus Christ our Lord. "Glory be to the Father, and to the Son, and to the Holy Spirit. As it was in the beginning, is now, and ever shall be, world without end. Amen."

Part One

Who Is Satan?

ONE

Satan in the Bible and Catholic Tradition

I N MY STUDIES FOR THE PRIESTHOOD, we seminarians were discussing the problem of evil in a class on moral theology. "What role does the devil play?" one of us asked. Our professor replied: "There is no such thing as the devil."

At that time, thirteen years ago, I believed there was a being called Satan, just as I had been taught in school. But here I was little more than a year away from being ordained, being taught there is no Satan—that no force or being other than human sin was responsible for evil in the world.

That is the stance of modern psychology, the scientific study of human and animal behavior, whose purpose is to understand, predict, and help control (that is, self-control) human behavior. There are as many different schools of psychology as there are ways of studying human behavior. Each can offer valuable insights into the human mind.

Think of your own life for a moment. Why do you act the way you do? Why do you say what you do? All of us respond to present-day situations according to our past experiences. For example, if in my childhood people had always told me I was no good and not lovable, I would have grown up with a poor self-image. Our experiences affect our beliefs about ourselves and the world.

The problem of evil is a complex one. In early 1991, the ABC television show *20/20* televised an exorcism.[1] At the conclusion was a debate by two Catholic priests, Frs. James LeBar and Richard McBrien. The latter stated that there is no being called Satan, that Satan is only human evil personified. All evil, he explained, is due to human decisions. Fr. LeBar, on the other hand, argued that Satan is an article of the faith of the Catholic church. He agreed that even though much evil is caused by people's choices, Satan is a real being who can affect human lives and cause evil in the world.

Which of these men is correct? Whose worldview is true? Is evil merely the result of human choices? Or is there an evil agent beyond humanity at work in the world? Is it "psychology against religion?" Or is it possible to unite psychological theory and religious conviction? Is belief in Satan just an old-fashioned superstition? Does modern psychology explain all that happens in the world?

The answers involve much study, prayer, and observation of human behavior. The starting point is to determine the nature of a human being. A human person is made up of a body, mind, and spirit. Because humans have physical bodies, they have limits. But they also have an intelligence that separates them from other animals. That part is the human mind. Each person has something special within him or her—something which calls each into an experience with a transcendent reality. That is the spirit of the person. In Catholic theology, it is called an immortal soul, the part of the person which is oriented toward God. The author of the book of Sirach teaches that when a person is conceived, God places a reverence for his holy ways within the person when he or she is in the womb (Sir 1:14). So being human also means being in relationship to God or desiring to be in relationship to him.

If anyone observing human behavior excludes any of these parts, the result will be a diminished view of humanity. This is an important consideration when seeking counseling. The whole person—body, mind, and spirit—must be explored if a therapist is to understand fully the person who has come for help.

Recently, I spoke with a therapist counseling adult victims of child abuse, who had noticed something peculiar in a number of her patients. As she explored the past with these clients, she began to question her own worldview. She believed in God, but did not practice any specific religion. The more she worked with these people, however, the more she realized there was something strange about them. Their experiences of child abuse had a different character than her other cases. Something evil was in them, an evil so horrible she could not explain it solely in psychological terms. Much evil can be directly attributed to choices that people make, but another evil has a more sinister character.

She shared her observations with some of her colleagues and discovered they were experiencing the same thing in their sessions with adult victims. They could not sufficiently explain the evil encountered with just psychology, but were looking outside the realm of their expertise to explain bizarre behaviors.

Where does a sound therapist turn to discover the source of such chilling, sinister evil? After studying the experiences of victims, he or she turns to God for revelation to understand it.

Beyond these examples taken from therapy and counseling, how can we even begin to explain in human terms the horrendous evil of the Nazi holocaust of World War II or more recently the Khmer Rouge genocide in Cambodia? Is it really conceivable that evil of this magnitude is merely human in origin?

The Bible tells us evil originated with the revolt of a heavenly angel called Satan: "Now war arose in heaven, Michael and his angels fighting against the dragon; and the dragon and his angels fought, but they were defeated and there was no longer any place for them in heaven. And the great dragon was thrown down, that ancient serpent, who is called the Devil and Satan, the deceiver of the whole world—he was thrown down to the earth, and his angels were thrown down with him" (Rv 12:7-9).

SATAN IS A FALLEN ANGEL OPPOSED TO GOD

This passage makes clear that Satan is an angelic being—that evil is not simply a lack of human goodness in the world. At its source is an angelic being called Satan. "The devil... is not to be regarded as a mere mythological personification of evil in the world; the existence of the devil cannot be denied."[2]

The proper name "Satan" first appears in Job 1:6-12, wherein Satan asks God's permission to roam the earth and to test Job (and, by implication, other followers of the Lord). Satan is not equal to God. He must ask permission from God. Satan is a created being and is therefore subservient to his Creator, God. He, with his followers, fell away from God and were thrust out of heaven.[3] Now he "prowls around like a roaring lion, seeking some one to devour" (1 Pt 5:8).

The Jews of biblical times believed in evil spirits. In Leviticus 16:6-10, the being Azazel is, according to most scholars, the name of a demon who inhabits the desert.[4] In Hebrew tradition, evil forces were not to be appeased. The people of God were to give honor only to the one true God. All contact with evil or demonic forces was explicitly forbidden. Hebrew prophets repeatedly described other religions as demon-controlled and insisted that any dalliance with them was idolatry.[5] Consulting with the gods of pagan nations, or demonic forces in Hebrew thought, was a very serious offense against the Lord.

But the angel of the LORD said to Elijah the Tishbite, "Arise, go up to meet the messengers of the king of Samaria, and say to them, 'Is it because there is no God in Israel that you are going to inquire of Baalzebub, the god of Ekron?' Now therefore thus says the LORD, 'You shall not come down from the bed to which you have gone, but you shall surely die.'" So Elijah went. **2 Kgs 1:3-4**

So we see that in the Old Testament the devil, Satan, is a reality. He was allowed to test Israel's faithfulness to God, but did not possess the same power as that of the Lord. God alone was sovereign and his will was to be obeyed. God called Israel to "be holy; for I am the LORD, your God" (Lv 20:7).

In the New Testament we receive a clearer understanding of the role of Satan in God's purpose. Jesus' earthly ministry demonstrates that he—that is, God in the flesh—came to free us from our sins and the grasp of Satan.

In the Gospels of Matthew, Mark, and Luke, Jesus prepares for his public ministry through his baptism at the River Jordan. In this act, Jesus is revealed as the leader of the new people of God, who are to find their identity as sons and daughters of the Father. In baptism, Jesus united himself with sinful humanity. He then began his ministry by a confrontation with Satan, known as the temptation in the desert. Jesus, full of the Holy Spirit, engages Satan on his own battleground and is the faithful witness (Rv 1:5), loyal to the Father (Mk 1:12-13; Mt 4:1-11; Lk 4:1-13).

After this victory, the Gospel of Mark indicates that Jesus called the first disciples. The Gospel of Luke reports that Jesus began to teach. The first sign (healing or miracle) of the power of Jesus is the casting out of a demonic spirit:

And immediately there was in their synagogue a man with an unclean spirit; and he cried out, "What have you to do with us, Jesus of Nazareth? Have you come to destroy us? I know who you are, the Holy One of God." But Jesus rebuked him, saying, "Be silent, and come out of him!" And the unclean spirit, convulsing him and crying with a loud voice, came out of him. And they were all amazed, so that they questioned among themselves, saying, "What is this? A new teaching! With authority he commands even t' unclean spirits, and they obey him." **Mk 1:23-27, parallel pass⸝ in Lk 4:33-36**

Since Jesus' first act is to confront Satan in the desert, and his first sign of power and authority is to cast out a demonic spirit, it is apparent that a primary purpose of his ministry was to expose Satan and destroy his power. Jesus' victory—which can be ours—is completed with his death and resurrection, and then coupled with God's sending of the Holy Spirit.

Jesus cast out demonic spirits many times in the Gospels, each time bringing a person freedom and healing. According to the New Testament, the demonic spirits of Satan also are real. (See Appendix One for Scripture citations.) If they were not, surely Jesus would not have dealt with them in such a way. I believe that to deny the existence of Satan and his demonic spirits is to deny the truthfulness of the Bible, that it is the inspired Word of God. After all, Satan plays a significant role in salvation history, in both the Old and New Testaments. The Bible, according to Vatican II, faithfully teaches us what we need to know for our salvation, and Satan is an important part of that revelation. He is not incidental to it.

Further, if one denies the existence of Satan and demonic spirits, he or she must question a significant part of Jesus' earthly ministry as recorded in the Gospels. At the very least, he or she must question Jesus' apparent understanding of these dark forces as demonic. For if they were merely psychological and physical in nature, this would show a lack of understanding, even ignorance, on Jesus' part. He evidently thought demons were real. And he differentiated between simply healing the sick and casting out demons. What would this view do to our conception of Jesus as the Son of God?

Affirming the Gospel record, the Catholic church in every age has believed in demonic spirits who are directed by a powerful personal being, Satan. He wishes to draw humanity away from the power and love of their Father, God. The early Church Fathers were concerned to protect Christians and those preparing for baptism from these satanic influences. They believed that the church was to continue the ministry of Jesus. And the proclamation of the kingdom of God included deliverance from the work of evil spirits. Justin Martyr writes that the ministry of healing and casting out evil spirits follows the example of Jesus, and that Christians are able to defeat the enemy through the power of Jesus' name.[6]

As the Gospel was preached in the early church, it was a given that Jesus' proclamation would be met with resistance from the evil one. An integral part of the church's proclamation includes prayers for healing and deliverance from evil spirits. St. Irenaeus writes that those who follow Jesus receive a special grace, which empowers them to drive out demonic spirits so people may be cleansed from evil, and thus prepared to be received into the church through baptism.[7]

It is evident that the early church waged war against evil spirits through individual and collective prayer. St. Ignatius of Antioch wrote to the Ephesians that they were to come together often and praise God, and thereby defeat Satan. Being a Christian meant joining Jesus in warfare against the devil.[8]

In the early church, a person wishing to be baptized was prepared through receiving a series of exorcisms, which took place after candidates registered their names.[9] Also prayer of casting out of evil spirits was common. Through the wisdom imparted by the Holy Spirit, the first Christians understood what Jesus was doing when he cast out evil spirits in the Gospels, and they believed that they were to continue this work. The theologian Origen emphasizes the spiritual power to be found in a simple prayer using the name of Jesus. He reminds his people that Jesus encouraged his followers to use the authority of his name. He teaches that when a follower of Jesus commands an evil spirit to flee, it must leave.[10]

THE CHURCH'S ABIDING BELIEF

The belief in the existence of the devil and demonic spirits does not end with the early years of the Catholic church. The Fourth Lateran Council (A.D. 1215) states, "For the devil and the other demons were indeed created by God naturally good, but they became evil by their own doing. As for man, he sinned at the suggestion of the devil."[11]

The Second Vatican Council repeats this teaching in several documents. The *Dogmatic Constitution on the Church* teaches that Satan is the one who deceives human beings and leads them away from God.[12] *The Constitution on the Sacred Liturgy* teaches that Jesus through his death and resurrection freed humanity from the power of Satan.[13] In the *Decree on the Church's Missionary Activity*, the Council teaches that Jesus was sent to rescue humanity from the power of darkness, thereby reconciling the world to God.[14] The church sends forth missionaries to free all the world's people from bondage to Satan and restore all of creation to the Lordship of Jesus Christ.[15] Finally, the *Pastoral Constitution on the Church in the Modern World* states that Jesus was crucified and rose to break the hold that Satan has on the world. Through his death and resurrection, the world can be made new, according to the plan of God.[16]

It is evident, from the Council's teaching, that my professor was wrong. There is a being called Satan—a being not equal with God, but subject to God. Evil is not merely a lack of human goodness. Real personal evil exists beyond the human realm. Followers of Christ are in daily struggle with "the principalities, against the powers, against the world rulers of this present darkness, against the spiritual hosts of wickedness in the heavenly places" (Eph 6:12).

Pope Paul VI in a general audience on November 15, 1972, stated that one of the greatest needs of the Catholic church at the present time was to be aware of the devil and his purpose: "This matter of the Devil and of the influence he can exert on individuals as well as on communities, entire societies or events, is a very important chapter of Catholic doctrine which should be studied again, although it is given little attention today."[17]

In its Rite of Baptism for children, the Catholic church expresses its belief in Satan. After the Litany of the Saints, the priest prays, "Almighty and ever-living God, you sent your only Son into the world to cast out the power of Satan, spirit of evil, to rescue man from the kingdom of darkness, and bring him into the splendor of your kingdom of light. We pray for these children: set them free from original sin, make them temples of your glory, and send your Holy Spirit to dwell within them."[18] Later in the rite, parents and godparents are asked to renounce Satan and all his works and machinations.

The Rite of Christian Initiation for Adults also contains prayers of exorcism that one needs to receive before being baptized. These are intended to free them from sin and the devil, and to give them strength in Christ. "Never let the powers of evil deceive them. Free them from the spirit of falsehood and help them recognize any evil within themselves,... In your love, free them from evil.... Command the spirit of evil to leave them, for you have conquered that spirit by rising to life."[19]

In 1975, the Sacred Congregation for the Doctrine of the Faith published *Les formes de la superstition* to help the faithful understand the church teaching regarding demonic spirits. Satan, it states, is not a product of the human imagination, but a real historical figure first described in the Bible and a key person in church doctrine. When someone says, "There is no Satan," he or she is denying part of the abiding faith of the Christian church, its way of conceiving redemption, and its very consciousness of Jesus himself.[20] To deny the existence of evil spirits is to deny, at least in part, the need for redemption which Jesus brought us through his death and resurrection. After all, an important component of that redemption is our deliverance from the evil one, not only deliverance from sin and death.

CONCLUSION

We can conclude the following:

1. If we want to understand the whole human person, psychological and physical views of personhood are not enough. We must consider the spiritual dimension of the human being.
2. Today counselors and therapists are discovering that in certain cases of adult victims of child abuse, there is an evil which is so horrible it cannot be explained solely in psychological terms, confirming the need to consider the spiritual dimension and possibly even the activity of supranatural beings. (Obviously, this is only one example of such sinister evil.)
3. The existence of a personal devil and evil spirits is a credible explanation, at least in part, for such sinister evil in the lives of human beings and the world as a whole.
4. The Bible, especially Jesus in the Gospels, confirms the existence of a personal devil who is active in the world.
5. In accord with Scripture, the Catholic church has consistently and constantly taught that there is a personal devil. This teaching is reflected in both the church's belief and practice.

But what are demonic spirits like? What is their purpose? How do they affect us? How much power does Satan really have? Can demons force us to do things? We will address these questions in chapter two.

TWO

Satan: His Nature and Activity among Us

For we are not contenders against flesh and blood, but against the principalities, against the powers, against the world rulers of this present darkness, against the spiritual hosts of wickedness in the heavenly places. Eph 6:12

I N EPHESIANS, is all of humanity engaged in a spiritual war? Yes! And Christians become soldiers in that battle upon their baptism.

In combat it's vital to know the enemy. Any good general knows his enemy's strengths and weaknesses. For Christians weakness is no different. So who *are* Satan and his demons? They are fallen spirits. The good angels are also spirits, but they are not demonic. We commonly call them angels. Some are messengers from God. The archangel Gabriel, for example, was sent to a town in Galilee named Nazareth, to a virgin... the virgin's name was Mary (Lk 1:26-38). Some minister to God, continually praising his name (Rv 8:2). God sends other angels to assist people in their walk with the Lord (Heb 1:14). The archangel Raphael was sent to help Tobiah (Tb 5:4). Demons, on the other hand, are messengers of Satan, their leader.

Angels and demonic spirits act differently. In the Bible angels do not wish to enter or possess a person or animal. Angels are content to do God's will. That is the opposite of the demonic spirits. They desire to inhabit or attach themselves to a body, whether human or animal, and possess it.

> They came to the other side of the sea, to the country of the Gerasenes. And when he had come out of the boat, there met him out of the tombs a man with an unclean spirit,... And when he saw Jesus from afar, he ran and worshiped him; and crying out with a loud voice, he said, "What have you to do with me, Jesus, Son of the Most High God? I adjure you by God, do not torment me.... My name is Legion; for we are many." And he begged him eagerly not to send them out of the country. Now a great herd of swine was feeding there on the hillside; and they begged him, "Send us to the swine, let us enter them." **Mk 5:1-12**

The demonic spirits did not want to leave the home they had become accustomed to in the Gerasene demoniac. They begged Jesus to send them into the swine, thus demonstrating that demonic spirits wish to inhabit or attach themselves to a bodily form, human or animal. If a demonic spirit is cast out and cannot attach to another human or animal, it will try to return to its former place of habitation (Mt 12:43-45).

Angels reside in heaven and follow the will of God. Demonic spirits rebel against God and reside either in hell or prowl the earth like roaring lions, looking for someone to devour (1 Pt 5:8).

In the Gerasene demoniac passage, one also realizes that demonic spirits have strong wills with which to bargain and struggle against Jesus. Though they resist, in the final analysis they must always be obedient to God's power (Mk 5:1-20).

Demonic spirits also identify with emotions. One expressed in the Gospels is fear (Mk 5:6-7). They have names as well. In the Gerasene story, they are named "Legion." Demonic spirits possess knowledge. In the first chapter of Mark one demonic spirit shrieks, "What have you to do with us, Jesus of Nazareth? Have you come to destroy us? I know who you are—the Holy One of God" (v. 24).

And in the fourth chapter of Luke, "Demons also came out of many, crying, 'You are the Son of God!'" (v. 41). Knowing that Jesus was the Son of God, the demons also knew that he had the power to destroy them. And so does anyone who is a true follower of Jesus because each has received this gift from the Lord.

Acts of the Apostles 19:13-16 shows how dangerous it is to try to use the power of the name of Jesus if one is not following him. The demonic spirits knew the faith of the Jewish exorcists. The demons even spoke to them. The demonic spirits knew who was commanding them to leave. They knew, for example, that these sons of Sceva were not followers of Jesus. On the other hand, they knew that St. Paul was a true follower and had the power to cast them out using Jesus' name (Acts 16:16-18). Demonic spirits can discern if a person is trying to follow the Lord's will with sincere devotion that leads to a deep relationship with him, or if he or she is a lukewarm Christian.

THE BATTLE IS DAILY

Daily struggle to follow the Lord Jesus naturally encompasses a battle against Satan and his demonic forces. Satan does not want a follower of Jesus to live in peace and harmony. Satan declares himself to be god and lord of the earth. His goal is to annihilate the followers of the Lord by seducing them away from God.

Let no one deceive you in any way; for that day will not come, unless the rebellion comes first, and the man of lawlessness is revealed, the son of perdition, who opposes and exalts himself against every so-called god or object of worship, so that he takes his seat in the temple of God, proclaiming himself to be God. Do you not remember that when I was still with you I told you this? And you know what is restraining him now so that he may be revealed in his time. For the mystery of lawlessness is already at work; only he who now restrains it will do so until he is out of the way. And then the lawless one will be revealed, and the Lord Jesus will slay him with the breath of his mouth and destroy him by his appearing and his coming. The coming of the lawlwess one by the activity of Satan will be with all power and with pretended signs and wonders, and with all wicked deception for those who are to perish, because they refused to love the truth and be saved. 2 Thes 2:3-10

Though Satan attacks the followers of Jesus in different ways, the Christian always must remember, "... neither death, nor life, nor angels, nor principalities, nor things present, nor things to come, nor powers, nor height, nor depth, nor anything else in all creation, will be able to separate us from the love of God in Christ Jesus our Lord" (Rom 8:38-39).

For the faithful servant of God, all Satan can do is harass one and make life difficult. Satan tries to deceive, entice, enslave, torment (bring into bondage), drive human beings away from God, or defile them even if they are baptized. (All human beings are called to be people of God.) A major tactic of Satan is to attack our minds and thoughts. He wants to deceive us for "... there is no truth in him. When he lies, he speaks according to his own nature, for he is a liar and the father of lies" (Jn 8:44). After a person hears the Word of God, "... Satan immediately comes and takes away the word which is sown in them" (Mk 4:15).

The followers of Jesus must always be alert because "the Spirit expressly says that in later times some will depart from the faith by giving heed to deceitful spirits and doctrines of demons" (1 Tm 4:1). To withstand satanic attacks on the mind, one must become fortified by the Word of God.

Not only does Satan attack our thoughts, but our physical well-being (Lk 13:10-13). Demonic spirits have the power to affect our senses and physical abilities. In Matthew 12:22-23, Jesus cures the possessed man by removing the spirit that possessed him. In Mark, a man brings his son to Jesus because the boy is possessed by a mute spirit (Mk 9:17). Also in Mark, the Syro-Phoenician woman ascribes her daughter's illness to an evil spirit (Mk 7:25-30).

St. Paul indicates that demonic spirits can harass anyone, even a member or leader in the church (2 Cor 12:7-9). Though an angel of Satan afflicted St. Paul, God allowed it so that the power of the Lord Almighty would be manifested.

When asked whether it was a blind man's sin or his parents' that caused him to be born blind, Jesus responded, "It was not that this man sinned, or his parents, but that the works of God might be made manifest in him" (Jn 9:3). So it may be with us.

Satan and his demonic spirits will use any means at their disposal to separate us from God. Even though Satan is powerful, even though Satan has an angelic intellect, he is not all-powerful or all-knowing. Satan does not know all our thoughts. There is only one Lord, Jesus Christ, who is all-powerful and omniscient. Satan's days are numbered. He is living on borrowed time. Jesus has conquered him for eternity.

He gives the power and authority over demonic forces to his people. Remember, the demons were subject to the seventy disciples (Lk 10:17-20). They were subject to St. Paul. They were subject to the first Christians. They also are subject to present-day followers of the Lord.

To use this power with wisdom and love, Christians must grow in developing a spiritual life which includes the sacraments of the church, daily prayer, and Scripture reading. In the Scriptures they will be taught how the Lord dealt with demonic spirits, how to use the authority of Jesus in this battle, and how demonic spirits operate.

Though defeated, Satan tries to show that he is strong. Though he will protest, even Satan must admit, "that at the name of Jesus every knee should bow, in heaven and on earth and under the earth, and every tongue confess that Jesus Christ is Lord, to the glory of God the Father" (Phil 2:10-11).

Christians are more than conquerors through the shed blood of Jesus Christ (Rom 8:37-39). War between nations demonstrates that even though the battle may be won, guerilla warfare can continue. That is what Satan wages today— guerilla warfare against Christians. To completely remove an adversary, the land must be cleared of all guerilla warfare, all pockets of resistance. The people of God are called to cleanse the world of Satan's pockets of resistance, his traps and deceptions.

God will protect ignorant Christians for a while in this conflict, but he expects us eventually to use our minds to discover Satan's snares. God desires enlightened Christians—a people who know his Word and are dedicated to him.

A STORY OF GOD'S PROTECTION

In the wee hours one morning, I received a call from the hospital, an emergency call for a priest. I dressed and started to drive over. I was at a red stoplight. Though it turned green, for some reason, I did not go. Just as I started to put my foot on the gas pedal, a car ran the red light, going about sixty miles per hour.

Had God not protected me, my car would have been broadsided. I might have been killed, or at least seriously injured. God had his hand on me. But God also calls me to obey the laws of the road when I drive. If I drive my car in ignorance of the traffic laws, I will do serious damage to myself and others.

The same principle holds for me in my life with God. God will protect me from the evil one for a while. But God expects me to learn about Satan's tricks so that I don't foolishly risk my life.

God, too, will protect his people from Satan's machinations for a time. But sooner or later, God challenges his followers to face Satan's deceptions head on. What are his tricks? What are his lies to deceive God's people? That is discussed in Part Two.

Part Two

Satan's Deceptions

THREE

Lie Number One: Divination

I HAVE LIVED IN FIVE CALIFORNIA PARISHES, two as a deacon and three as a priest. I have lived in East Los Angeles, the center of Los Angeles, Pomona Valley, San Fernando Valley, and Camarillo. If you were to drive through these parishes, you might note they have something in common. All have a growing number of signs that say: Palm Reader, Fortune Teller, or Spiritual Advisor. The people who run these establishments are involved in divination.

Divination is a pseudo-science of predicting future events or exploring past events through occult means. Such diviners are seeking knowledge that is not attainable through human or godly means. Knowledge comes either from God, from human beings, or from Satan. In divination, is one asking Satan for knowledge? God? Or human beings? The ouija board is but one form of many divinations.

THE OUIJA BOARD

A woman came to me for psychological counseling because ten years before she and a friend had used the ouija board. She said that she had contacted the spirit of an Indian princess, who would answer all their questions. She could feel this presence even as we spoke—the same presence that she had felt when using the ouija board. She had come into bondage with the spirit of the Indian princess. My client came into bondage because she sought knowledge, not from God, but from a spirit that she contacted using the board. She was freed when I prayed to break the bondage through the power of the name of Jesus.

Who was this Indian princess? Was she a demon? Was she the spirit of a deceased person? Or was she a higher self-consciousness? To answer these questions let's look at the history and purpose of the ouija.

Ouija is a game where one asks the board questions and expects to receive answers. The board "was used in the days of Pythagoras, about 540 B.C. According to a French historian's account of the philosopher's life, his sect held frequent séances or circles at which 'a mystic table moving on wheels, moved towards signs which the philosopher and his pupil, Philolaus, interpreted to the audience as being revelations supposedly from the unseen world.'"[1]

Ouija-like instruments were used in China before the birth of Confucius as a non-threatening way to communicate with the spirits of the dead.[2] Ouija instruments also were popular in the third century A.D., in Rome. In France in 1853, a spiritualist named M. Planchette devised an instrument similar to the ouija board that Parker Brothers manufactures today.[3]

Elijah J. Bond designed a variation of the board in America in 1891. William Fuld bought the rights from him a year later and filed for a patent. In 1966, Parker Brothers purchased the rights and are the current manufacturers of the ouija board.[4]

Though the ancient purpose of the board was to contact spirits of the deceased, its modern-day makers state that people can use it to search their unconscious self for answers to questions.

The commerical board is made of pressed cardboard and

imprinted with letters of the alphabet and numbers. A little platform on it has a glass center. The person places his or her hands upon this platform. After the questions are asked, the players allow their hands to move with the platform, spelling out the answer to their questions. Historically, the ouija board was believed to put players, not in touch with their unconscious, but with a being. This being is one of two: either a person who has died and is not at rest with the Lord, or a demonic spirit.

Some people who use the ouija board, such as my client, become obsessed with using it. One may begin by asking simple questions. After a time, the person may rely on the board for every decision. This is bondage. It is possible to be in bondage to a ouija board, just as one can be in bondage to money or possessions. Through the ouija board a person opens the door to deeper experiences of the occult.

So whom did my client contact? It was not her higher self-consciousness. It could have been a demonic spirit. Such spirits have knowledge and can imitate the voices and appearances of people who have died. Or it could actually have been the spirit of someone who had died. First Samuel 28:8-17 tells the story of King Saul going to the witch at Endor to conjure the spirit of Samuel. God may permit an occasion like that for a specific reason, but it is clear in the Bible that we are not to try to contact the dead.

THE TAROT

Another popular method of divination is the use of tarot cards. The pack consists of seventy-eight cards. Fifty-six are contained in four suits, forming the minor arcana. The twenty-two others are picture cards, called the major arcana.[5] This group comes from Hermes Trismegistus, councilor of Osiris, King of Egypt,[6] and are frequently related to cabala. (See section on the cabala in chapter seven for more information.)

The twenty-two cards of the major arcana are the key to the tarot. They correspond to the the letters of the Hebrew alphabet.[7] A study of the major arcana reveals many beliefs of those who follow the cabala. This makes it highly probable there is a connection between the major arcana and the cabala. By laying out the tarot cards in a diagram of the Tree of Life (see chapter seven on the cabala for the Tree of Life), anyone experienced in using the tarot for divination can attempt a complete life reading of a person.[8]

The specific intent of reading tarot cards is to gain a knowledge about someone or events in that person's life that is not possible through humans or God. Tarot card readers claim that the cards are magical: "Anyone, with a certain amount of application, can learn to read the cards with skill. But one who has more than the usual psychic and psychological insight can bring to the reading a broader, deeper, more subtle understanding. *The Magic Is in the Cards.*"[9]

Some centers of spirituality use the major arcana cards for Christian meditation. This movement has as its basis an ancient work by Hermes Trismegistus. Unfortunately, the people who are supporting it neglect to explain that Hermes Trismegistus is the Greek name for the Egyptian god Thoth.[10] One should not mix such tools and Christian meditation.

The tarot is part of the occult. It is wrong to use the cards for any purpose. They should not even be in the house of a follower of the Lord.

PALMISTRY

Palmistry, also called chiromancy or handology, is the study of the human hand, which, of course, is a distinct part of the human body. It is true that some conclusions about a person can be made through the study of the hand. For example, there are hands that appear to be sensitive and artistic, while others appear to be firm and strong-willed. But that is as far as one can go.

In palmistry, or palm reading, one tries to tell the future.

"The hand is divided into areas and lines. There is the lunar mountain, the Venus belt, the Martian plain, and areas for spirit, fortune, success, fame, imagination, will, and sensuousness. Further, there are four lines which dominate the surface of the palm: the head line, the heart line, the profession line, and the life line. From these indications palmists claim to divine and foretell the future."[11] Palmistry, when used for telling the future, is another method of fortune-telling, which is forbidden in the Scriptures (Dt 18:10).

ROD AND PENDULUM

In the ancient world, people tried to predict the future through the use of the rod and pendulum, which have their roots in pagan soothsaying.[12] The priests of the Israelites were warned against its use in Hosea: "My people inquire of a thing of wood, and their staff gives them oracles. For a spirit of harlotry has led them astray, and they have left their God to play the harlot" (4:12).

In using pagan methods for divination, the Israelites were disobeying the first commandment. Their sin was idolatry. They had abandoned the Lord.

The book *Christian Counseling and Occultism* explains that the rod and pendulum serves the same purpose as a medium (a person who leads a séance). The use of these articles has its origin in pagan religions.[13] They become most dangerous when used in the practice of spiritism. As in the use of the ouija board, the conversation with the dead person (or demonic spirit) is accomplished through an alphabet table. The pendulum selects the letters which, when properly arranged, spell out the answer to a question.

ASTROLOGY

Every bookstore carries numerous books on astrology. Newspaper tabloids in supermarkets use astrology to make predictions of the future. In the daily newspaper, readers can find their "horoscope for the day." The signs of the zodiac (astrological signs) are popular items for jewelry. Some people will marry only a person with a compatible astrological sign. Does being born under a certain astrological sign determine who we are?

Astrology is the forecasting of earthly and human events by observing and interpreting the fixed stars, sun, moon, and planets.[14] It originated in Mesopotamia as part of a religion that identified various gods with particular heavenly bodies.[15] Constellations were distinguished, including the twelve signs of the zodiac. Its original purpose was to inform the king or nation of a course of action, based on the positions of the planets and of the zodiacal signs.

In the Hellenistic period (third century B.C. to third century A.D.), Greek astrology developed. They applied astrology to the lives of individuals.[16] It flourished as a religion because it offered a causal explanation of everything. Astrology continued to be recognized as a science until the eighteenth century.

Though fundamentally opposed to astrology, the early church had difficulties fighting it because astrology permeated the entire culture. St. Paul writes, "See to it that no one makes a prey of you by philosophy and empty deceit, according to human tradition, according to the elemental spirits of the universe, and not according to Christ" (Col 2:8). To combat astrology, the church, "by calling Christ the 'sun of justice' (a phrase derived from Mal 4:2), substituted him for *Sol* (Sun). In the fourth century, the church went even further and decided to celebrate Jesus' nativity on December 25th, the birthday of the sun, when 'lux crescit.'"[17]

Even though astrology was condemned by a papal bull in the 1590s, it remained popular. Its practice as a religion sharply declined with the invention of the telescope. New planets and thousands of stars were discovered, destroying the apparent primacy of the traditional constellations so that the astrological system broke down. "By the 17th century... astrology lost its intellectual viability and became scientifically untenable. Though Kepler attempted to devise a new method of computing astrological influences in the heliocentric (Sun-centered) universe, he did not succeed, since no astral influences are possible in a Newtonian universe."[18]

Western astrology, though of great interest sociologically and popularly, has no intellectual merit.[19] This is an instance where science has verified what the sacred Scriptures and the church have taught, though it was not strong enough to follow its own pronouncements. Belief in astrology is not compatible with the Christian life.

NECROMANCY

A popular movie in 1990 was *Ghost.* Whoopie Goldberg, playing a medium, allows the spirit of a dead person to occupy her body and thus commmunicate with a living person. Her routine was to ask a "client" a question, then communicate with the spirit of the dead person and relay the answer.

To try to keep a relationship with someone who has died is not psychologically healthy. Relatives and friends must let go of the beloved, even though it is natural to feel sad and mourn the loss of a loved one.

A British psychiatrist, John Bowlby, contends people form attachments for safety and security. Bonding begins at birth, usually moving from parents to friends and spouses, and undergirds people throughout most, if not all, of their lives. This is normal.

George Engel, a psychiatrist affiliated with the University of Rochester, believes the loss of a loved one is as traumatic psychologically as a severe wound is physically. Just as it takes time to heal the physical wound, so with one that is psychological.

Think about the last time a friend of yours died. How did you feel? Now recall the death of someone you loved deeply. Did you react differently? Most likely, because of the intensity of the bonding.

Mourners need to complete the basic steps of the grief and healing process, which may take from four months to five years. If they do not, they may become psychologically unbalanced.

Persons going to a medium to communicate with their deceased loved ones block recovery, to their detriment. Going to a medium harms not only themselves, but others who are close to them. But people also go to mediums to get advice. They may also want to know what the future holds.

Necromancy comes from the Greek words meaning "dead" and "divination." It is the practice of attempting to foretell the future through communication with the dead. Today necromancy is called spiritualism, spiritism, or channeling. It takes many different forms. It has already been shown that in its early ages, the ouija board was a tool for necromancy.

Channeling (spiritism, being a medium, a psychic, or whatever you wish to call it) supposedly involves achieving an expanded state of consciousness that allows one to connect with a high-level guide or higher source of self.[20] These guides claim they are beings of light who wish to help. These high-level guides warn that there are also lesser-evolved entities and caution that one needs to learn how to tell such entities apart.

The guides claim that they come from the causal plane, a very high vibratory dimension where you can exist only after you have harmonized your life-energies. They add that most souls live in the astral plane: "There is a level of reality one frequency or step removed from yours called the 'astral plane' where many souls go in between earth lifetimes."[21]

The higher guides caution against contacting these souls, but that if one contacts them instead, the person will experience peace and love, for they are here to serve humanity. They declare they are "beings of light," because they have evolved into spirit and have taken on the shimmer of light.[22] But do these guides really wish to serve humanity? Could they be something else in disguise? Remember: "for even

Satan disguises himself as an angel of light" (2 Cor 11:14). Are these guides from Satan? Are they angels? Whatever they are, José Silva believes that they are harmless.

Silva was born on August 11, 1914, in Laredo, Texas. He grew up doing odd jobs to help support his family. He never went to school, except to teach. His brother and sister taught him how to read and write. He first became interested in the workings of the mind while he was in the Signal Corps, where he read the writings of Freud, Jung, Adler, and other prominent therapists. At the same time he studied metaphysical writings and parapsychology. He experimented with hypnosis, trying to improve the human memory. Silva eventually abandoned hypnosis and began developing mental training exercises, which included relaxed concentration and vivid mental visualization as ways of reaching lower levels of brain wave activity. From these exercises evolved Silva Mind Control.

Today Silva Mind Control is promoted as a technique that teaches a person how to gain conscious control of subjective levels of the mind normally associated with the unconscious. Its ultimate goal is to reach oneness with Reality—the pantheistic deity of which all creation is believed to be composed.[23]

The beginning stages of Silva Mind Control seem innocent. Unfortunately, the farther one progresses in it, the deeper one becomes involved in occult practices. In the middle of the basic four-day course, students learn how to project their beings into spaces (for example, into their own living room at home). This is astral projection, an occult practice. Then they are encouraged to project themselves into plants, animals, and finally other human beings. This is dangerous because it breaks the person's psychological integrity.

The greatest danger of Silva Mind Control is when participants are asked to build their own laboratory and invite counselors to assist them in their lives. "In his laboratory he evokes two counselors, a man and a woman. He is told before he begins this meditation session that he will do this and, if he is like most other students, he will have a pretty firm idea of who he wants as counselors."[24]

But who are these counselors? "Counselors can be very real to Mind Control graduates. What are they? We are not sure—perhaps some figment of an archetypal imagination, perhaps an embodiment of an inner voice, perhaps something more."[25] Perhaps something more. Perhaps the spirit of someone who has died and is not at rest with the Lord. Or perhaps a demonic spirit.

José Silva has the same dilemma as the spiritist, medium, necromancer, or channelor. Silva states that the source of the information one receives through using Silva Mind Control is not God. "I have mentioned Higher Intelligence a number of times in past chapters. Is this some noncommittal way of mine of referring to God? I cannot prove what I am about to say; I must speak from faith. My answer is no, by Higher Intelligence I do not mean God. I use capitals for the words because I am so respectful of it, but to me it is not God."[26]

One must ask, who or what is this "Higher Intelligence?" It is not God. It is not human. What about the spiritist, medium, and channelor? Whom are they contacting? Christians must turn to God's Word for the answers.

DIVINATION AND THE BIBLE

Divination, whether from the ouija board, tarot cards, palmistry, rod and pendulum, astrology, necromancy, channeling, Silva Mind Control, or any other form, is forbidden in the Bible. It is a serious offense because in practicing divination, one is seeking knowledge from a supernatural source other than God.

The prophet Hosea equates divination with adultery, telling his people that when they turn to pagan methods of divination they are like an adulterer, an unfaithful wife (Hos 4:9-12). The piece of wood and the wand that Hosea mentions in this passage are tools for divination.

When you come into the land which the LORD your God gives you, you shall not learn to follow the abominable practices of those nations. There shall not be found among you any one who burns his son or his daughter as an offering, any one who practices divination, a soothsayer, or an augur, or a sorcerer, or a charmer, or a medium, or a wizard, or a necromancer. For whoever does these things is an abomination to the LORD; and because of these abominable practices the LORD your God is driving them out before you. You shall be blameless before the LORD your God. **Dt 18:9-12**

To practice divination is to disobey the first and foremost commandment, to follow the one, true God. Divination is, in fact, a rebellion against God (1 Sm 15:23). God has a covenant with his people, and he expects them to keep it. "Do not turn to mediums or wizards; do not seek them out, to be defiled by them. I am the LORD your God" (Lv 19:31). The prophet Zechariah also cautioned his people to refrain from all types of divination. Diviners, he says, speak nonsense (Zec 10:1-2).

Practitioners of divination are not sent from God. They are among the prophetic voices of the pagans, and the people of God are to pay no heed to them. Jeremiah told his people just that.

The consequences of participation in divination can be very serious. King Saul, for example, disobeyed the Lord in numerous decisions he made, but the most serious offense was when he sought an oracle from the witch of Endor, a sin which contributed to his death (1 Chr 10:13-14).

The consequence of King Ahaziah's consultation of Baalzebub also was death (2 Kgs 1:1-4,17). Consultation or inquiry of a demonic being or deceased person, rather than God, is expressly forbidden. Israel was destroyed because its people had forsaken the one, true God and followed pagan practices, including divination:

And they burned their sons and their daughters as offerings, and used divination and sorcery, and sold themselves to do evil in the sight of the LORD, provoking him to anger. Therefore the LORD was very angry with Israel, and removed them out of his sight; none was left but the tribe of Judah only.

Judah also did not keep the commandments of the Lord their God, but walked in the customs which Israel had introduced. And the LORD rejected all the descendants of Israel, and afflicted them, and gave them into the hand of spoilers, until he had cast them out of his sight.

2 Kgs 17:17-20

The Jewish race had rebelled against the law God gave them in Deuteronomy 18:10-12. The sins of Manasseh, the most evil king of Israel, mentioned in 2 Kings 21:6 are: "And he burned his son as an offering, and practiced soothsaying and augury [divination], and dealt with mediums and with wizards." King Josiah, on the other hand, "put away the mediums and the wizards... that he might establish the words of the law which were written in the book that Hilkiah the priest found in the house of the LORD" (2 Kgs 23:24).

Does God forbid knowledge of the future? No, he doesn't. God sends prophets into the world to warn and guide his people. Look in the Bible. God clearly gave the prophets messages. God sends special people, called saints and mystics in the Catholic tradition, who sometimes receive special revelations from God. Even today, many Catholics believe that God is sending Mary to us through various apparitions. (Keep in mind that such messages from Mary and various saints are private revelation and need not be believed, even though they may be approved by the church. They are not on the level of Scripture and Tradition, which is public revelation.)

A person may say of divination, "I do it just for fun, just to see what it is like." Would a person put his physical life in danger "just for fun"? Moreover, this "fun" can provide entrance for Satan into one's life. A snowball does not carry much weight to it, but if that snowball is rolled down a large, snow-covered hill it increases in size. The same is true with occult involvement. It starts small, but if unchecked, it can become a serious problem.

Have you or someone you know become involved in divination? One simply needs to repent and renew his or her relationship with the loving God. Jesus forgives anyone who comes to him, sincerely asking forgiveness. No matter how many times a person transgresses the will of God, his forgiveness is assured.

Janet, whose story is in the next chapter, was not involved in divination. She didn't believe people could contact the dead. But she did have a lot of problems and was looking for something to help her. Going to church seemed an empty experience, even though she believed Jesus was her Lord. Still, something was missing. She explored different religions, but none seemed to help. Then one day a friend brought her to a special class. Would it give Janet the answers she was seeking?

Transcendental Meditation

JANET'S CLASS WAS TAUGHT BY an experienced yoga master from India. Besides showing her postures and breathing techniques, he gave her a mantra to repeat to help her meditate. For fifteen minutes a day she meditated, using a picture of Jesus as her focus while repeating her mantra.

One day she heard the words: "Get rid of Jesus." She stopped, wondering who had spoken. She tried to meditate again, and again she heard: "I said, get rid of the picture of Jesus."

This experience caused Janet to stop meditating, but whenever she went into the room she had used for meditation she was overcome with a cold, eerie feeling. When she came to me for counseling, I was led by the Lord to break the bonds of any spirit guides that might have attached themselves to her, which brought her great relief and peace.

Even so, Janet was still unable to find peace in the room where she had meditated. She tried to read Scripture there, but couldn't. One of her daughters did not even want to enter it.

Finally, she called and asked me to bless her house. I experienced a coolness in a corner of the room. It was not a

peaceful coolness, but evil. "Is this where you used to meditate?" I asked. "Yes, this is where it happened," she replied.

I asked the Lord to remove the cool, evil presence and fill
the space with his peace. I asked him to send angels to remove
anything that was not from him. Something lifted. A great feeling of warmth swept the place. Janet and her family have had
no problem going into that room since the blessing.

Janet had unknowingly become involved in Transcendental Meditation (TM). While looking for peace in her life,
she found fear. Janet was innocent. She didn't know that her
meditation was not from God. But the evil one does not care
whether she or anyone else is ignorant.

Christian meditation is helpful. Reflection on the Scriptures is good, as is reflection on the Stations of the Cross, and
the lives of Mary and the saints. But Catholics, and all Christians, must be discerning. The meditation of a Benedictine
monk is different from the meditation of a Hindu yogi.[1]

Meditation is a mental discipline of concentration, a way
of centering inwardly. "It (meditation) necessitates reaching
a state of inner relaxation, an integration of body-soul-spirit
into a wholeness so that the meditator can direct that level of
increased inner awareness to whatever end he is seeking....
The Christian will look on meditation or concentration as a
means to move into prayer where he becomes progressively
freed from his habitual preconditionings of sense impres-
sions, emotional responses, and intellectual and volitional
patterns. He moves to a level of freedom in deeper faith to
communicate with God with greater obedience and loving
submission."[2]

Both meditation and hypnosis take a similar approach, but
each has a different motivation in directing the person's consciousness, as he or she reaches a state of concentration. In
hypnosis one yields to the suggestions of the hypnotist, while
in Christian meditation one searches for union with God.
The person is surrendering heart and mind to God, no matter how relaxed he or she becomes. Dr. Herbert Benson, a

cardiologist of the Harvard faculty of medicine, demonstrated that the brain wave activity during hypnosis and prayerful meditation was not the same, proving a difference exists between the disciplines.[3]

TM is the abbreviation for the system of meditation made popular by Maharishi Mahesh Yogi of India. Though presented as the way to inner peace and happiness, it is more than just a meditation technique. It is a religion. "Yet one who knows anything about Hinduism of the Shankara type can discover the basic tenets of a religion in the suppositions that underpin the whole philosophy behind TM. These basically are that all things are united as a whole and that through initiation a person can raise his consciousness to a level where he can touch this unity in all things and realize his oneness with the impersonal, ultimate Being."[4]

TM itself can never get to the core of one's problem. It can only give temporary relief from tension. Massive uncontrolled anxiety can be released through using TM, which the person must deal with or risk the fragmentation of personality. But the greatest danger is possible contact with the demonic. When a person empties the psyche (mind), something comes in to fill that emptiness. "Nature abhors a vacuum." When you empty a glass of water, air fills the glass. When a person empties his or her psyche, something will fill it.

TM removes the barriers that keep in balance destructive tendencies in the unconscious. Through TM the evil one can work in and through people or enter the physical world directly.[5] That is what happened to Janet in the beginning of this chapter.

Probably the TM user who uses the technique only to relax will not be influenced by evil spirits. But those who use TM to reach different levels of consciousness for a long period of time are in real danger of contacting demonic spirits.

Dr. Elmer Green of the Menninger Foundation of Topeka, Kansas, has studied the workings of the psyche in deep meditation. He reports:

According to various warnings, the persistent explorer in these... realms... brings himself to the attention of indigenous beings who, under normal circumstances, pay little attention to humans.... They are of many natures and some are malicious, cruel, and cunning, and use the emergence of the explorer out of his previously protective cocoon with its built-in barriers of mental and emotional substance as an opportunity to move, in reverse so to speak, into the personal subjective realm of the investigator. If he is not relatively free from personality dross, it is said, they can obsess him with various compulsions for their own amusement and in extreme cases can even disrupt the normally automatic functioning of the nervous system, by controlling the brain through the chakras.[6]

Jill came to me for spiritual direction. She was involved in the Cursillo movement, and her prayer life was growing. But sometimes she felt uneasy. She would feel peace when she prayed, but she wondered, "Am I really communicating with God?" She had been involved in TM for eight years. She had received many prayer mantras. Some of the feelings that she experienced while praying to God, she had also experienced to a degree in TM. She was confused and afraid. She knew she had been deceived by TM, but she also doubted her own Christian prayer experiences.

I believed that she needed to renounce her involvement in TM in the name of Jesus. I led her in a prayer of renunciation. Then I anointed her with blessed oil. When the oil touched her forehead, she began to move her head in a long circular motion. I placed my hand on her shoulder and prayed that she would be freed from all involvement in TM. I asked Jesus to send St. Michael the Archangel to remove all influences of TM and any spirit guide that she had received through TM. She began to shake uncontrollably. She tightly grasped my hand that was on her shoulder. She was bouncing up and down in the chair. I continued to pray. After about forty-five seconds, she stopped shaking. She was calm. I asked Jesus to remove her doubts about her Christian prayer. She was freed from a bondage to TM through the power of Jesus Christ.

MEDITATION THAT IS CHRISTIAN

I recommend that you use a way of meditation that is Christian. Using the Jesus Prayer or the Prayer of the Heart is a good place to start. It centers the person on God and God alone. The prayer originated in an Eastern Christian spirituality called *hesychasm*,[7] which requires a journey into the "heart." In scriptural language the heart is the seat of human life, the very depths of personality. All persons are commanded to love God with their whole heart, their whole soul, and their whole mind (Mt 22:37). When we seek God with all our heart, we will find him (Jer 29:13).

In the sixth century, at the center of hesychasm, the Monastery of St. Catherine on Mount Sinai, monks experienced a very personal, warm devotion to Jesus through the simple repetition of his name. A common form of this is the Jesus Prayer: "Lord, Jesus Christ, Son of God, have mercy upon me, a sinner."[8] The devout repetition of the name of Jesus, as St. Paul encouraged, can bring us into a deeper union with God (Phil 2:9-11).

"The emphasis in this prayer is upon the awesomeness and transcendence of Jesus Christ as Lord. Also in this prayer, persons acknowledge that they are sinners and in need of redemption."[9] When persons lose their sense of sinfulness, they also have lost the need for a Redeemer.

St. Gregory of Sinai in his *Instructions to Hesychasts* gives instructions to the faithful on how to pray the Jesus Prayer. He warns that sometimes people can tend to be lazy when praying. Praying the Jesus Prayer does take a certain amount of effort. It is not good to change the words or phrase of the prayer. Rather choose a phrase (either the whole prayer, or a shorter version like "Jesus, Son of God, have mercy on me") and be consistent with that phrase. In the beginning of the prayer it is good to say the prayer with both the lips and the mind, being careful not to disturb one's concentration by praying too loudly. Eventually the mind will become accustomed to this style of prayer. The deeper roots of this prayer in the power of the Spirit will then be evident to the person.[10]

A person should not be afraid to use the Jesus Prayer (or any other ejaculatory Christian prayer) throughout the entire day. A few minutes of praying in this way can bring greater peace in a time of stress and trouble. It is wise to have a spiritual director whenever using a prayer that employs psychosomatic methods of relaxing, as the Jesus prayer does. It is not good to learn a meditation technique from a Zen or Hindu master or TM instructor and then transfer the technique over to a so-called Christian mantra.

Three years ago a woman came to me who learned a meditation technique from a Zen master. She said that in his teachings to her he prayed over her, laying his hands upon her head. She felt an electricity go through her body in this experience. When she came to me for prayer and counseling, I had to break the bondage that had occurred due to that experience. After I broke all ties to the Zen master in the name of Jesus, she experienced a peace and inner freedom.

Remember—the call of Christians is to holiness, not to a relaxation technique. We are to center upon God, his indwelling life within us. This is done within the context of the Catholic church's teachings which are given to guide us and strengthen us. The Jesus prayer also helps us concentrate on our need for God's forgiveness and mercy.

Christians are called to seek the glory of God and surrender to his holy will. They are not to seek a self-satisfying psychic experience in prayer.[11] The final criteria of whether a person is growing in holiness in prayer are the fruits of the Holy Spirit. "The fruit of the Spirit is love, joy, peace, patience, kindness, goodness, faithfulness, gentleness, self-control" (Gal 5:22).

In meditation, keep in mind that Christians can also benefit from reflecting on the Psalms or any Scripture, as well as the Stations of the Cross or other Catholic devotions. The Catholic prayer of the Rosary is a good way to meditate on events of Jesus' life. Many different chaplets—that of the Holy Spirit, St. Michael, St. Joseph, and other saints—can be used for meditation. With an abundance of prayer techniques in our Christian tradition, there is no need to turn to TM for inner peace. True peace is possible only in union with the one true God.

According to an article in the January 7 edition of the *Los Angeles Times* in 1984, "An intense fantasy game between two teen-age brothers ended when one fatally shot the other with a gun they had found in the house." How could such a tragic incident occur among brothers playing a mere fantasy game? You'll hear more about this incident in the next chapter on witchcraft.

FIVE

Witchcraft

A WORD WHICH HAS MEANT ONE THING in a previous generation can have a different meaning now. For example, the word "gay." Not too long ago, it meant happy or excited. A gay party was a lively one. Today gay has a different connotation. A gay person is a homosexual and a gay party is for homosexuals. Words can change meanings.

That is what has happened to the word witchcraft. Once, witchcraft signified an art similar to satanism. This is also called black witchcraft—witchcraft in the traditional sense of the word. Today witchcraft also can denote a pagan folk religion called Wicca, or what is called contemporary witchcraft. This chapter treats witchcraft in the traditional sense. Chapter seven will cover Wicca.

Generally, people have a desire to be in control of every aspect of their lives. In performing witchcraft, people hope to gain mastery of others and the world around them through spells and curses. Witchcraft is different from magic. Many anthropologists define magic as the manipulation of an external power by mechanical or behavioral means to affect others; and witchcraft as an inherent personal quality that is used to the same ends.[1] In this definition, the word sorcery is synonymous with magic. A distinction also must be made between stage magic and sorcery (magic). Stage magic is a magic of illusion and is neither sorcery nor witchcraft. In stage magic one is not seeking the help of an invisible reality to gain control of others or the world around oneself.

Both witchcraft and sorcery have four elements. These elements are: performance of rituals or prescribed symbolic gestures, use of material substances and objects that have symbolic significance, utterance of a closely prescribed spell or of a less formal address, and a prescribed condition of the performer. Each element affects the power of a spell.

The purpose of the magic will determine the type of ritual used, as well as the day and time of the ritual. Certain types of spells require particular herbs. Some herbs are used on certain days of the week to enhance the spell's power. The words of the spell are very important too. Sometimes they are written down to obtain more power. The person performing the ritual must desire it with all his or her might to obtain the greatest effect, even sometimes fasting for twenty-four hours before to purify the body.

The propensity to be a witch or warlock is usually attributed to heredity, or at least is considered constitutional in the sense of having been implanted through one's generational heritage.[2] (Remember, this is traditional witchcraft, not Wicca. In Wicca anyone can be a witch through study and practice.) A person can also have the propensity to become a witch through being magically dedicated as a child to an evil spirit by an adult family member. No single description of a witch or warlock is common to all societies, but most believe witches have animals and birds as their familiars, or imps.

Witchcraft and sorcery date back to ancient Mesopotamia and Egypt. The Old Testament makes it clear that the Israelites and their pagan neighbors were aware of magic and witchcraft. In Exodus 7:11, Pharoah "summoned the wise men and the sorcerers; and they also, the magicians of Egypt, did the same by their secret arts."

Witchcraft and sorcery imply belief in an invisible reality.

Their use brings one into bondage with that invisible reality. According to the Bible, that invisible reality is not God, but an evil entity (Dt 18:12).

The admonitions against witchcraft and sorcery in the Old Testament must be understood in the light of the first commandment: "I am the Lord your God... You shall have no other gods before me" (Ex 20:2-3). In witchcraft and sorcery, a person is seeking assistance from a supernatural being other than God. That is why Exodus 22:18 states: "You shall not permit a sorceress to live." Though these practices of witchcraft and sorcery were prohibited, many of the Jewish people were not mindful. "Woe to the women who sew magic bands upon all wrists, and make veils for the heads of persons of every stature, in the hunt for souls! Will you hunt down souls belonging to my people, and keep other souls alive for your profit? You have profaned me among my people for handfuls of barley and for pieces of bread, putting to death persons who should not die and keeping alive persons who should not live, by your lies to my people, who listen to lies" (Ez 13:18-19). The bands and veils represent sorcery, barley and the crumbs, types of divination. The innocent who die are the human sacrifices. King Manasseh encouraged infidelity to God by immolating his sons by fire in the Valley of Ben-hinnom. He practiced augury, divination, and magic, and even appointed necromancers and diviners of spirits, so that he provoked the Lord with the great evil that he did in his sight (2 Chr 33:6).

Malachi 3:5 declares that sorcery is against the law of God. Micah, too, warns his people that if they continue practicing witchcraft their cities will be destroyed (Mi 5:9-13). Jeremiah also cautions the people not to listen to diviners, soothsayers, and sorcerers (Jer 27:9).

The New Testament similarly prohibits witchcraft and sorcery. In Acts of the Apostles, Simon Magus was practicing magic, but he was envious of the apostles when he saw the people receive the Holy Spirit through their laying on of hands. He offered them money to teach him how to do it, to which Peter said: "... your heart is not right before God. Repent therefore of this wickedness of yours..." (Acts 8:9-22). Practicing magic and following the laws of God are incompatible.

St. Paul called Elymas, the magician, an impostor and a fraud, a son of Satan and enemy of all that is right (Acts 13:9). Because Elymas was trying to prohibit the spread of the gospel and practicing magic, he was blinded by the Lord. Those who practice sorcery are in danger of not inheriting the kingdom of God unless they repent (Gal 5:19-21; Rv 18:23; 22:15).

DUNGEONS AND DRAGONS

Dungeons and Dragons® [3] (D&D) is Fantasy Role Playing (FRP) which requires that a person use his or her imagination and assume some role in fantasy play. The historical setting is the middle ages but with a twist of ghoulish fantasy. The D&D game set contains a rule book, some graph paper, and an odd set of dice. Through rolling the dice players determine their character's personality, age, diseases, parasitic infections, special skills, race, and class. Then each player rolls to determine his or her character's "hit points," that is, the damage that can be sustained without being killed. Players also receive a set amount of gold to buy weapons. Participants choose their character's "alignment" from three possibilities: Law, Chaos, or Neutral. Each has good and evil characteristics—that is, lawful good, lawful evil, chaotic good, or chaotic evil.

The Dungeon Master is the most important person in the game. The DM is usually an experienced player who draws up the game board. The DM also is the only one who sees the map of the maze and places monsters selected from the rule book. He or she not only directs the players, but makes all final decisions. Players enter the dungeon and battle the monsters while seeking treasure, trying to survive. No real end is reached and a typical session can last from four to twelve hours. A person's adventures end when his or her character is killed.

In many D&D games players may fantasize committing murder, arson, torture, rape, or highway robbery.[4] Examples from the D&D monster manual are:

Harpy: The Harpys attack, torture, and devour their charmed prey. What they do not want they foul with excrement.

Lizard Man: They are omnivorous, but lizard men are likely to prefer human flesh to other foods. In this regard they have been known to ambush humans, gather up the corpses and survivors as captives, and take the lot back to their lair for a rude and horrid feast.[5]

The following excerpt from the critical hit table demonstrates how graphic the fantasy of violence can become in D&D:

Dice roll: 37-38; hit location: crotch/chest; results: genitals/breast torn off; shock.

Dice roll: 95; hit location: guts ripped out; results: 20 percent chance of tangling feet, die in 1-10 minutes.

Dice roll: 100; hit location: head; results: head pulped and splattered over a wide area.[6]

Fantasy power can be a strong attraction to many who feel powerless in the real world.

The most powerful weapons in D&D are usually magic and witchcraft, so players will want to obtain and use them. As they learn spells, they are actually learning some of the rudiments for witchcraft. In the *Dungeon Master's Guide,* "There are directions for chanting, the use of familiar spirits, speaking with the dead, uses of occultic symbols to protect the spell caster, and definitions of special spells used by shamans and witchdoctors."[7] Magic and witchcraft, in some form, are found in all FRP rule books.

Many of the spells, incantations, symbols, and protective measures are genuine occult techniques. For example, in many spells, before the player recites the incantation, he or she draws a protective circle around the body—exactly as real-life witches do. D&D teaches some of the basic terms of the occult.

D&D presents a worldview that is not compatible with Christianity. Everything in the game is treated as a *fantasy,* even casting spells. The Bible, on the other hand, tells us that witchcraft and magic can be *real,* not just fun and games. The follower of God is to have no part in them.

D&D regards good and evil as equal forces. As a result, good and evil deities are seen as equal in power. In opposition to D&D, good and evil in the Bible are not equal forces. Jesus Christ, through his death and resurrection, has defeated Satan. Jesus is the all-powerful Lord. God will always triumph over evil.

I believe that the most insidious aspect of D&D is the way it can undermine belief in Jesus Christ as *the* Son of God. Remember that in D&D all characters are treated as fantasy, including gods, devils, and demons. Jesus Christ himself is one of many gods in D&D. Consider the possible chain of logic for a vulnerable teenager: D&D is just a game. The monsters aren't real. The gods aren't real. Jesus Christ is a god in D&D. Therefore, according to D&D, Jesus Christ is not real.

The testimony of the Holy Spirit in John 16 speaks to a Christian's heart, telling each of us that the basic sin of humanity is the refusal to believe in Jesus, that he has triumphed in death and returned to the Father, and defeated Satan through the power of the cross.

D&D is not to be confused with the fantasy of fairy tales. Though fairy tales contain witches, warlocks, witchcraft, and magic, their heroes are usually normal human beings. Only the evil people in them use magic or witchcraft. The human heroes, though tempted to use witchcraft or sorcery, usually do not. They typically use human means to achieve their ends. As Lewis' and Tolkien's mentor G.K. Chesterton pointed out, the genius in fairy tales lies in the fact that the hero is a normal person in an abnormal world, an innocent among ravaging nether beasts.[8] If the hero in the fairy tale is an abnormal person, as is the case many times in D&D, the entire meaning of the fairy tale can change.

In summary, from a Christian perspective, D&D can be a dangerous game. Its philosophical basis is contrary to the Christian worldview. D&D tends to be graphically violent in its fantasy play. It can also be dangerous because it may intensify psychological problems in some players, or may even be linked to an act of violence by troubled teenagers. Consider the following account from the *Los Angeles Times:*

> An intense fantasy game between two teen-age brothers ended when one fatally shot the other with a gun they had found in the house.
>
> Oakland police homicide Detective Jerry Harris said this weekend that the New Year's Day shooting of Juan DeCarlos Kimbrough, 14, by his 15-year-old brother, Anthony, was ruled accidental.
>
> The brothers were playing "Dungeons and Dragons," a fantasy game set in medieval times that involves role-playing and magic. Juan had assumed the role of "dungeon master," a powerful individual who directs the play of the game.
>
> Investigators said Juan had wrapped his character in an

invincible cloak and directed his brother to test its protective powers with the gun.[9]

Aside from such an admittedly extreme incident as the one above, D&D can be dangerous because it may become an entrance into the occult through its teachings and practice of magic and witchcraft. Inasmuch as it treats Christ as a fantasy character and as one among many gods, D&D may undermine the faith of Christians who play it. For a follower of Jesus Christ, there is no good reason to role-play fantasy characters who regularly practice magic and witchraft which God condemns.

Linda noticed something happened every time she wore a turquoise bracelet from her aunt. Did it have a curse or spell on it? Was there really such a thing? We discuss Linda's plight and that of others in the following chapter on sorcery.

SIX

Sorcery

THE LEGEND OF FAUST tells the story of a person who made a pact with the devil. Faust, a German magician and astrologer, desired knowledge and power, but could not obtain them by himself, so he sold his soul to a demon, Mephistopheles. While Faust himself is legendary, the gist of the story's meaning is certainly true—some people will do anything, even make a pact with the devil, to get what they want.

Contemporary sorcery is not understood as selling one's soul to the devil. It can be practiced by anyone who acquires the necessary magical substances and spells. In sorcery, a person is trying to influence human or natural events through an external force to effect a "magical result." This force, though invisible, is real. Beyond ordinary human capabilities, this supranatural power is not the all-powerful God, but an evil reality as explained in the previous chapter.

Sorcery works through things. For example, music, charms, talismans, amulets, certain incantations, pieces of clothing, drugs, special rites, and images. Even jewelry can be a part of sorcery, so people should be careful what they place on their wrists or around their necks.

Historically, sorcery has been used for both public and private purposes. Public use of sorcery or magic, as it is commonly called, is "official sorcery." For example, in ancient times, and in some countries today, rites are performed to bring rain to relieve a severe drought, or perhaps guarantee a good harvest.

"Private sorcery," on the other hand, is used in secret by individuals or groups. Some people categorize private magic, calling destructive magic "black" and protective magic "whi·*e." Black magic they call sorcery, and white magic simply magic. While this distinction may seem correct in the material world, it is not in the spiritual. All magic, whether black or white, is dependent upon interaction with a supranatural reality outside God's sanctioned limits for human beings. That reality is not God but the evil one, regardless of the outcome. Therefore, all magic, whether used to help or harm someone, is tainted. That is why it is accurate to call magic what it really is: sorcery. (Remember I am not referring to stage magic. Please see previous chapter.)

All four types of sorcery use symbolism. No firm boundary exists between one type and another. Rather, the boundaries are fluid. *Object sorcery* operates on the principle that by obtaining a part of a person—that is a bone, hair, nail, or even a piece of clothing—one can affect the welfare of that person.

A *contagious sorcery* is the magical effect gained through touching power-laden objects, such as stones, animals, and plants. Touching or holding the object transfers power to an individual. An example of *contagious sorcery* is the belief that a lion's tooth contains the power of the lion. When worn as an amulet, the tooth transfers the strength it contains to the wearer.

In *sympathetic sorcery* the magical causal sequence is due to the sympathetic capacity of the human person.[1] Once this relationship is established, the desired magical effect is accomplished. For example, when a hunter draws a picture of his prey in the sand and then strikes it, the hunter seeks assurance of a successful hunt. *Sympathetic sorcery* also is used when a person obtains a picture of another person and curses it. Some religions curse little figurines or "dolls" that represent human beings. The Western world calls these figurines voodoo dolls. Contemporary sorcery calls them poppets.

The last type of sorcery is *gnosiological,* which works on the intellectual sphere. To be proficient in this type, one must know the magical constellations of the universe and how they are harmonized. Also you must know what god to invoke for certain needs and what each requests in return for the desired effect. *Gnosiological sorcery* is the basis for modern theosophy.

Sorcery, like witchcraft, must be understood in the light of the first commandment: "I am the LORD your God.... You shall have no other gods before me" (Ex 20:2-3).

I've indicated that sorcery can work through things or objects. Some objects *do* carry a blessing from God. For example, a crucifix carries with it a grace or power to draw people to God when used in the proper way. A statue of Mary or of a saint can inspire devotion to following God's will. The use of sacramentals (blessed salt, water, oil, or a candle) can bring grace. Likewise, some objects can carry a curse or a bondage to Satan. A style of music, for example, can lift one's heart and mind in praise of God, while another can glorify Satan. Some songs speak openly of rebellion against God. The spiritually perceptive Christian realizes that this style of music repels the presence of the Holy Spirit.

DRUGS AND OBJECTS IN SATANISM OR SORCERY

Satan also uses drugs. These open the unconscious mind to suggestions. When a person is in a drugged state, demonic music filters into the unconscious and the words and rhythm of the songs become imbedded in the unconscious. Drugs combined with demonic music can result in bondage to Satan and eventually lead to deeper problems.

Talismans are man-made objects endowed with a magical power to bring about good or evil. They can be made of any material, but traditionally some substances are more appropriate than others. For example, for the greatest effect, a love talisman should be made from copper.[2] A talisman also has an inscription—words or a design whose meanings are described in some occult books. The most common is a metal disc worn on a chain as a pendant. On one side is a personalized design and on the other, an inscription.[3]

An example of a talisman is the ceramic eye which Armenians give a newborn baby on a small chain to protect the infant from harm. By contrast, in Italian culture, the eye is evil and places a curse on a child. To offset a curse, Italians claim a horn is quite effective because the horn has its own curse.[4] It is said to protect the child from the evil eye because it bears an even greater evil.

An amulet is not man-made, but comes from nature. Common amulets are a bear's claw and a rabbit's foot. Were the amulet engraved and consecrated, it would be a talisman.

If objects that carry the presence of Satan are in a Christian home, a spiritual battle will take place there. Artifacts depicting pagan gods in a home may invite certain spiritual forces to enter. If a crucifix carries within it a blessing from Jesus whom it depicts, then it follows that replicas of Aztec, African, and Eastern gods (including replicas of Buddha) may carry within them a certain power.

Celia grew up in the Philippines, where her mother had a statue of Buddha in their house. When Celia was experiencing some problems, her mother, after taking her to church, had her kneel in front of the statue and pray for help. When I prayed to break all her ties to Buddha and set her spirit free to follow the one, true God, she experienced great release and inner peace.

People should be careful with the possessions that they have in their homes. A Christian's home is to be dedicated to the Lord. The presence of the Holy Spirit is to dwell within such homes.

Linda, a third grader, had received a turquoise bracelet from her aunt. Every time that she wore it something bad happened. One day her mother asked her why she did not wear her aunt's gift any more. When Linda cried and explained, her mother gave the bracelet to her parish priest, who placed it on the altar during his next celebration of

Mass. Linda was then able to wear the bracelet with no problems. The power of the Mass had broken the evil that had been placed upon that turquoise bracelet.

SYMBOLS OF EVIL

People involved in satanic cults, as well as satanists (people who worship Satan as god, but are not in cults), usually possess items bearing satanic symbols. They frequently draw them on paper, walls, and road signs; they might draw or tattoo them on their skin.

Satanic symbols also can be found on jewelry, to remind devotees of the evil spirit they follow. Just as a follower of God might wear a cross or crucifix, a satanist might wear a satanic symbol on an article of clothing. Some are used in conjunction with incantations to invoke the presence of Satan.

Following are some common satanic symbols that Fr. Joseph Brennan explains in his book, *The Kingdom of Darkness:*

Pentagram:
Each point represents one of the elements of the universe. The star also symbolizes humanity, the top point being humanity reaching toward the heavens, the bottom tow points being humanity straddling the natural world. The symbol is said to conjure up evil spirits.

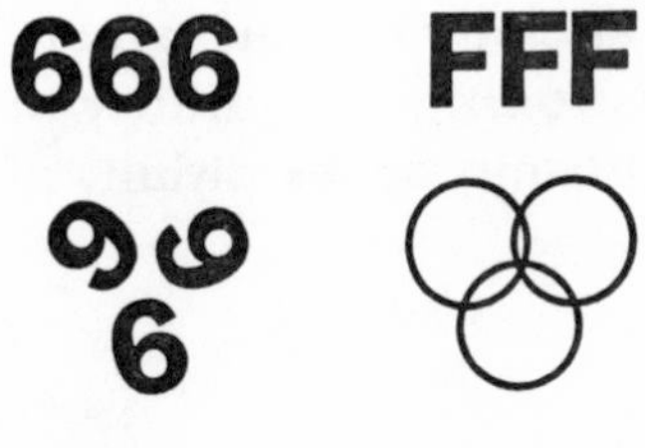

Mark of the Beast
The mark of Satan, the Beast, the Antichrist, is made in four ways. In the last book of the Bible, Revelation, Chapter 13, the number of the Beast is revealed as 666.

Goathead:
Symbolizing the horned goat, the goat of Mendes, the scapegoat, this is one of the satanist's ways of mocking Christ as the Lamb who died for the sins of humanity.

Upside-Down Cross or Southern Cross:
A mockery and rejection of the cross of Christ, this emblem is worn by many satanists and can be seen on some rock musicians appearing on heavy metal music album covers.

Broken Cross or Peace Sign:
This sign represented peace in the 1960s, but now among occult groups it represents the hoped-for defeat of Christianity—another way of mocking Christ.

Satanic Cross or Cross of Confusion:
An ancient Roman symbol questioning the validity of Christianity or the divinity of God.

Satanic S or Broken S:
This represents a thunderbolt and means "destroyer." It was worn by members of the feared death squads of Nazi Germany.

Scarab beetle:
This is the dung beetle, which is the ancient Egyptian symbol of reincarnation. It is also symbolic of Baalzebub (Satan), Lord of the Flies. It is worn in the occult to show that its holder has power, and it is said to be a source of protection from others within the occult realm.

Udjat or All-Seeing Eye:
A symbol that refers to Lucifer, the king of hell. The eye is half closed, illustrating that even though you may not think the devil is watching you, he is. Below the eye is a tear, because he "mourns" those outside his influence.

Horned Hand:
This is a sign of recognition among those who are in the occult. It may also be used innocently by those who identify with heavy metal music, as well as fans of the Texas Longhorns athletic teams.[5]

SANTERIA

Santeria is a religion that has its origins with the Yoruba tribe of Africa. The Yoruba lived in what is known today as Nigeria, along the banks of the Niger River. At one time they had a powerful and complex social structure organized in a series of kingdoms, the most important of which was Benin.[6] The kingdom of Benin lasted from the twelfth century until 1896.

In the late eighteenth and early nineteenth centuries, the Yoruba waged a series of disastrous wars with their neighbors and among themselves.[7] The internal fighting and the external attacks led to the downfall of the Yoruba people and the eventual enslavement of many of them. Between 1820 and 1840, the majority of slaves shipped from the ports of the Bight of Benin were Yoruba.[8] These slaves were brought to Cuba and Brazil to work in the sugar plantations. Due to the hundreds of sugar mills, the demand for slaves was enormous.

The Yoruba were quick to establish a strong community in Havana. Spanish law insisted that slaves be baptized as Roman Catholics as a condition of their legal entry into the Indies. The religious laws of Catholic Cuba guaranteed the slaves rights of private property, inviolable marriage, and personal security. The Yoruba came to be called "Lucumi" after their way of greeting each other, *oluku mi,* "my friend."[9]

In the light of history, the Catholic church failed to Christianize the Lucumis. Even though the church did baptize them, which gave them certain civil rights, its leaders did not properly instruct the Lucumis. Although the church did not intend to keep the religion of the Lucumis alive, it did through its policies of recognizing ethnic diversities.

The Catholic practices of the Spaniards deeply influenced the Cuban Lucumis. The popular piety of Catholicism in Cuba was centered almost exclusively on the veneration of the saints. In their efforts to hide their magical and religious practices from the Spaniards, the Lucumis identified their African deities with the saints of Catholicism.

This was the beginning of Santeria.[10]

The deities that the Yoruba brought with them from Africa have been syncretized with the Catholic saints. (A proper understanding of Catholic saints will be given later in this chapter.) For example, the greatest feast for the Afro-Cuban population was the celebration of Epiphany. It was special because of the legend of Melchior who came from Africa to adore the Christ child. Afro-Cubans found their role in Catholic society by identifying with this African presence in the Christian folklore.[11] At Epiphany the Lucumis brought an African flavor to the celebration of the Christian feast. They did this with all the special feasts of saints. These celebrations allowed the Lucumis to be both Catholic and African, and to continue worshiping their gods.

The Lucumis gradually adapted to complement and reflect the Catholic worldview. Through this accommodation emerged Santeria, the way of the saints, because the devotions to the *orishas* (African gods) were carried out beneath the images of the Catholic saints. In this new religion a Catholic saint and a Lucumi *orisha* were seen as different manifestations of the same spiritual entity.[12]

Santeria came to the United States in 1959, the time of the Cuban revolution. Since that time over one million Cubans have left the island as political exiles. Among these people were *santeros*, priests and priestesses of Santeria. They established the ways of the *orishas* in Puerto Rico, Venezuela, and particularly in the American cities of Miami and New York.[13]

Santeria worships a central, creative force called *Olodumare.* He is the ultimate destiny of all creation; from him all existence comes forth, and to him it all returns. *Olodumare* expresses himself in the created world through *ashe. Ashe* is the blood of cosmic life, the power of *Olodumare* toward life, strength, and righteousness. It is a divine current that finds many conductors of greater or lesser receptivity.[14] *Ashe* is the absolute ground of reality.

Olodumare created the *orishas* to manifest his will and

express his essence in nature. They are personifications of *ashe*. The *orishas* also are the guides and protectors of the human race.[15] A central belief in Santeria is that each person's life is overseen by a specific *orisha*. The *orishas* take an active part in a person's everyday life. As said earlier, a follower of Santeria believes that the Catholic saints are simply manifestations of the *orishas*. When *santeros* say that the pale virgin whom Catholics know as Saint Barbara is Shango, they are saying that what we see is a picture of a *camino* (a manifestation) of Shango, that is, Shango incarnating himself through a pale white woman who is his vehicle.[16]

Generally, *santeros* honor the Catholic saints in the Catholic manner, reciting prayers in Spanish, and worship before the *orishas* in the African manner, using Lucumi. The following is a chart of the *orishas* and the Catholic saints with whom they are syncretized:

Orisha	Saint	Principle
Agayu	Christopher	fatherhood
Babaluaye	Lazarus	illness
Eleggua	Anthony of Padua	way-opener
Ibeji	Cosmas & Damian	children
Inle	Rafael	medicine
Obatala	Our Lady of Mercy	clarity
Ogun	Peter	iron
Olokun	Our Lady of Regla	profundity
Orula	Francis	wisdom, destiny
Osanyin	Joseph	herbs
Oshosi	Norbert	hunt, protection
Oshun	Our Lady of Caridad	eros
Oya	Our Lady of Candelaria	death
Shango	Barbara	force
Yemaya	Our Lady of Regla	maternity[17]

In Santeria, on the feast day of one's *orisha*, one must attend both the Catholic Mass and the ceremonies of that *orisha*. One of the basic differences between the saints and the *orisha* is that the saints are not offered sacrifices, or *ebbo*, like the *orishas*.

The *orishas* need the *ebbo* to live. Therefore, they are not immortal. The theory behind all Santeria sacrifice is that the *orisha* consume the invisible *ashe* of the sacrifices that is instilled in or, better, liberated from them, through consecration, the sacred words of the *moyuba* dedication.[18]

The *ebbo* consists of special herbs and the blood of sacrificed animals. Each *orisha* has his own herbs and animals which he enjoys consuming, and only those things which the *orisha* enjoys should be sacrificed to him. The blood and herbs are poured over special stones which represent each *orisha*. In the ancient myths the *orisha* left the primordial community of Ile-Ife by descending into the earth. All that remained of their presence were stones, still resonating with their *ashe*.[19] These special stones contain the spiritual essence of the *orishas*.

There are three types of animal sacrifices: an offering for cleansing from evil or from a curse, an offering to an *orisha* for assistance, and an offering for an initiation ceremony into one of the orders of Santeria. Before any *ebbo* can be offered, a person must first propitiate the *eggun* and *Eleggua*. The *eggun* are the spirits of one's ancestors: "They include not only the spirits of relatives, but also the dead santeros mayores—that is, the elders who belonged to the same 'house' or 'family' in which one has been initiated.... Among the *eggun* are those spiritual entities that were assigned to an individual as his guides and protectors when he was born."[20] *Eleggua* is the *orisha* who carries the offerings to the other *orishas*. He will not do so unless he is honored first.

The *santeros* and *santeras* are the priests of Santeria. They are able to assist the people in their prayers and offerings to the *orishas*. Another name for them is *omo-orisha* because during the ceremony in which they become *santeros* they dedicate themselves to an *orisha*. The ceremony in which a person becomes a *santero* is called the *asiento*. In this ceremony an *orisha* forms a special bond with the *santero*. After receiving

the *asiento,* a person may continue in the heirarchical structure of Santeria by being initiated in the *pinaldo* or *cuchillo.*
This is the sacrificial knife. Only those who have received the
cuchillo may perform the animal sacrifices.

The high priests of Santeria are the *babalawos.* They are
the master *santeros.* In a difficult case, a *santero* turns to the
babalawo.[21] The *babalawo* seeks information through divination. There are three forms of divination in Santeria: the
opele, the *table of Ifa,* and the *ikin.* The opele "consists of an
iron chain that connects eight oval medallions usually made
of coconut rinds, although they can also be made of tortoise
shell, ivory, bone, copper, or tin. The *babalawo* interprets the
oracle according to which sides of the eight medallions fall
down when he throws the *opele* on his working table."[22]

According to the *babalawos,* the *table of Ifa* contains all the
wisdom of the world—past, present, and future. The *table of
Ifa* is a round wooden tray. A special powder known as *eyero -
sun* is sprinkled on it. Then the *babalawo* uses a deer horn to
draw the lines and zeros which represent the oracle. In *Ifa* a
person is seeking knowledge of one's destiny or the future.
This divination reveals the presence of psychic forces around
the person and whether those forces are good or evil.

The most important of the oracles are those that use the
ikin, the sacred palm nuts.[23] This system uses sixteen palm
nuts for divination. In Santeria at least three *babalawos* are
required to interpret the *ikin.*

Once the *babalawo* has determined if a curse has been
placed upon someone, or if an evil has been attached to
someone, his responsibility is to remove the curse or cleanse
the person of the evil. If through the processes of divination
good is discovered attached to a person, the good must be
reinforced.

The first of the initiations received in Santeria is that of the
necklaces, known as the *elekes.* Five necklaces are given, which
belong to Eleggua, Obatala, Shango, Yemaya, and Oshun.[24]
These are given for protection against evil. To receive this initiation, persons must first receive a *limpieza,* or cleansing, to

purify them. Afterwards, they are expected to respect the *orishas* and live a decent and moral life.

Santeria's most basic belief is that destiny begins before birth in *Ile-Olofi,* the house of God in heaven.[25] It is from there that each person receives his or her destiny. Those who do not fulfill it will be punished by the *orishas* and must reincarnate until their duties have been accomplished.

As one studies Santeria, it becomes clear that Santeria is rooted in pagan divination and sorcery. Its priests use divination to discern the destiny of an individual and the causes of his or her problems. Sorcery—that is, magic—is then used to encourage a good destiny or to cleanse the person from evil. The rituals are accompanied by sacrifices to the *orishas*—an offering of herbs and plants or an animal sacrifice.

A Catholic must be particularly wary of Santeria because it tries to blend some aspects of Catholicism with its beliefs. For example, a woman from El Salvador spoke with me after Mass, saying she had visited a neighborhood botanica or Santeria store. Since it contained traditional Catholic articles, she thought it was okay to buy anything there, so she purchased a red necklace. Unfortunately, that necklace had been dedicated to the orisha Shango and carried with it his protection. Her chain was carrying not a blessing, but a curse. Satan does not care whether she knew what she was doing. He uses anything he can to draw a believer away from Jesus Christ.

It is very easy for Catholics, especially those of the Latin culture, to be deceived when they walk into a botanica and see traditional saints and articles next to Lucumi orishas. Let's examine the great difference between the saints and the orishas.

SAINTS VERSUS ORISHAS

The Catholic church has the tradition of honoring people as saints who have followed the call of God in an exemplary way. The church states that saints are definitely in heaven, yet never in its history has it worshiped the saints as if they were God.

The word worship comes from the Old English *weorthscipe*, which means the condition of being worthy of honor, respect, or dignity. In the older sense of the word, to worship means to give someone honor, whether that person be a government official or God. The highest worship, or highest honor, is given to God alone. The honor given to persons or saints is different from that given to God. In some older Catholic writings one finds the term "worship of the saints." There the word worship is being used in its original sense, that of giving honor. Today the word worship has the connotation of adoration. That is why today it is improper to use the term worship in referring to the saints. The proper term is veneration or honor.

To show honor to someone is common. In the United States a justice of a court is addressed "Your Honor." In marriage vows one promises to "love, honor, and obey." People who have died for their country are honored. People are honored for heroic deeds. Our government leaders receive honor because of the office they hold. And in Scripture one reads: "Honor your father and your mother" (Ex 20:12). There is nothing wrong with giving people honor whether they are living or deceased, especially if the deceased are before the throne of God praising him.

In the Scriptures, angels are honored (venerated). Joshua honors an angel who is the captain of the host of the Lord: "When Joshua was by Jericho, he lifted up his eyes and looked, and behold, a man stood before him with his drawn sword in his hand; and Joshua went to him and said to him, 'Are you for us, or for our adversaries?' And he said, 'No; but as commander of the army of the LORD I have now come.' And Joshua fell on his face to the earth, and worshiped, and said to him, 'What does my lord bid his servant?'" (Jos 5:13-14).

The prophet Daniel honors an angel who brings him a message: "When I, Daniel, had seen the vision, I sought to understand it; and behold, there stood before me one having the appearance of a man. And I heard a man's voice between the banks of the *Ulai*, and it called, 'Gabriel, make this man understand the vision.' So he came near where I stood; and when he came, I was frightened and fell upon my face. But he said to me, 'Understand, O son of man, that the vision is for the time of the end'" (8:15-17).

In Tobit one reads:

"I am Raphael, one of the seven holy angels who present the prayers of the saints and enter into the presence of the glory of the Holy One."

They were both alarmed; and they fell upon their faces, for they were afraid. But he said to them, "Do not be afraid; you will be safe. But praise God for ever. For I did not come as a favor on my part, but by the will of our God. Therefore praise him for ever." Tb 12:15-18

The saints are united with God. They are before the throne of God because they see him as he is. "Beloved, we are God's children now; it does not yet appear what we shall be, but we know that when he appears we shall be like him, for we shall see him as he is" (1 Jn 3:2).

When a family member dies, the family usually keeps pictures or mementos of him or her. These mementos help to remind the living members of the life that was lived. As they look upon their dear one's likeness, they remember moments they shared and how the person lived and their *dedication to God*. The same is true with the saints. They are our brothers and sisters, members of the family of God.

Pictures and statues in Catholic churches are not gods, but simply representations of the saints to remind us of their dedication to the one true God. "The fact that someone kneels before a statue to pray does not mean that he is praying to the statue, just as the fact that one kneels with a Bible in his hands—as fundamentalists at times do—does not mean that he is worshiping the Bible. Statues or paintings or other artistic devices are used to recall to the mind of the person the thing depicted. Just as it is easier to remember one's mother by looking at her photograph, so it is easier to recall the lives of the saints, and thus be edified by their examples, by looking at representations of them."[26]

Death does not mean someone is no longer alive. Death means that the person is not here on this earth and thus can no longer be seen. Those who have died and are in heaven are alive to God. "... Have you not read in the book of Moses, in the passage about the bush, how God said to him, 'I am the God of Abraham, and the God of Isaac, and the God of Jacob'? He is not the God of the dead, but of the living." (Mk 12:26-27). The saints are in heaven before the throne of God. In the account of the transfiguration Moses and Elijah appeared in glory and spoke with Jesus. When Peter saw this he said, "Master, it is well that we are here; let us make three booths, one for you and one for Moses and one for Elijah" (Lk 9:28-34). While Peter's timing was inappropriate, the intent of the booths was to honor Jesus, Moses, and Elijah.

Just as people on earth pray for one another, so the saints in heaven, who are members of one's spiritual family, pray for the people of God still on earth. At death people are not cut off from one another but have a different bond, a bond in the Lord. This is what the Catholic church calls the communion of saints.

This term, which is also called the Mystical Body of Christ, expresses the common bond that is shared by those who are in communion with God. How the bond is created is explained in the Gospel of John: "I am the vine, you are the branches. He who abides in me, and I in him, he it is that bears much fruit, for apart from me you can do nothing" (Jn 15:5). Those connected to Christ are also connected to one another. Those who have died and are in heaven are still connected to Christ. They are not cut off from the vine. The saints remain branches. Therefore they remain related to the people of God on earth.[27]

This relationship is also expressed by St. Paul in 1 Corinthians 12:12-27. Paul explains that the people of God are united, just as the body is united. If one part is suffering, all the members suffer with it. If one member is honored, all are honored with it. The people of God share a mystical union with one another through Jesus Christ. "For as in one body we have many members, and all the members do not have the same function, so we, though many, are one body in Christ, and individually members one of another" (Rom 12:4-5).

A natural, even necessary inference from this teaching is intercessory prayer. St. Paul asks, "I appeal to you, brethren, by our Lord Jesus Christ and by the love of the Spirit, to strive together with me in your prayers to God on my behalf" (Rom 15:30). Hebrews 13:18 encourages the faithful to pray for the leadership of the church.

The saints are branches of the vine of Jesus Christ in heaven. The followers of God on earth, the branches of the vine on earth, are encouraged to intercede for one another. Therefore, the saints, still members of the vine, can intercede for the followers of God on earth. The saints in heaven pray for the saints of God on earth.

The angels and saints also can place the prayers of the faithful before the throne of God: "And so, when you and your daughter-in-law Sarah prayed, I brought a reminder of your prayer before the Holy One; and when you buried the dead, I was likewise present with you" (Tb 12:12).

People can honor saints by praying to them, that is, asking for their intercession. This is similar to asking a friend here on earth to pray for their needs. When a person asks for a saint's intercession, the saint brings the intentions of this person to God. "And when he had taken the scroll, the four living creatures and the twenty-four elders fell down before the Lamb, each holding a harp, and with golden bowls full of incense, which are the prayers of the saints" (Rv 5:8).

"And another angel came and stood at the altar with a golden censer; and he was given much incense to mingle with the prayers of all the saints upon the golden altar before the throne; and the smoke of the incense rose with the prayers of the saints from the hand of the angel before God" (Rv 8:3-4).

Jesus himself alluded to the possibility of intercessory prayer. In Luke 16:19-31, the rich man is seeking help from Lazarus. He first asks for personal comfort. Then he asks for Lazarus to help his family so that they will follow God. This asking for assistance is a type of prayer, seeking the intercession of Lazarus.

We see, then, that there is a valid role for the saints in heaven as intercessors, and we are to honor them as holy men and women who have gone before us. But the power and authority come from God alone, and not from sorcery of any kind.

Lucy was not involved in witchcraft or sorcery, but she was depressed. Her parents thought that I might be able to help her. Lucy had tried something that sounded new, but was a variation on an old theme.

SEVEN

New Age and
Neo-Pagan Movements

L UCY, TWENTY-FOUR YEARS OLD, had been suffering from depression for three years. She told me she had gone to a
special meeting whose leader said she had different energy
centers in her body. To feel good about herself, she would
have to invite energy into these centers.

Lucy tried the exercises, breathing different colors of light
into her body: red, yellow, orange, green, blue, indigo, and
violet. They were supposed to free her from depression and
fear. She watched Elizabeth Clare Prophet, the guru of this
group, on television and followed her exercises too. She did
not get better.

I explained to Lucy that this meditation was not based on
God and gave her a choice: choose Jesus or Elizabeth Clare
Prophet. When she could not give up her light breathing
exercises and Prophet, I encouraged her to seek therapy and
gave her some referrals. I don't know if she ever contacted
them, but sooner or later each of us must answer the same
question I asked Lucy: Is Christ the answer or not?

Lucy had become involved in a cult of the New Age Movement (NAM). The cult is the Church Universal and Triumphant (CUT). What is NAM (New Age Movement)? Where
does it come from? What are its teachings?

91

The New Age Movement is best understood as a network, an extremely large, loosely structured collection of organizations and individuals bound together by common values and a common vision.[1] Though NAM is not part of satanism, it does contain elements of the occult. Practicing of NAM spirituality opens the door to involvement in the occult.

NAM promotes ecology. Its members seek inner peace. NAM envisions global harmony. How can such an organization be an open door to the occult? To understand the dangers of NAM it is essential to look at its foundations and beliefs.

New agers believe that "all is one"—everything that exists consists of one and the same reality. This Ultimate Reality is neither dead matter nor unconscious energy. It is being, awareness, and bliss.[2] This is the Hindu description of God. The New Age has its roots in ancient Sumerian, Indian (Buddhist and Hindu), Egyptian, Babylonian, and Persian religious practices.

All that is, is God (which is pantheism). Human beings are part of "all that is." Therefore, human beings are divine.[3] This is monism. There is no difference between God, a human person, a carrot, or a rock. They are all part of a continuous reality that has no boundaries, no ultimate divisions.[4] The New Age god is vastly different from the God revealed in the Bible.

New Agers believe that people are separated from their divinity only in their consciousness. They are ignorant of their divine reality. To become aware of their divinity, they need to alter their consciousness and so experience oneness with the divine. Through techniques of altering consciousness one comes to the realization that one's true self is God.[5]

This experience, in turn, will lead to personal transformation. Personal transformation will lead to planetary evolution and global harmony. As people experience their own divinity, the world will be changed and humanity will enter the "Age of Aquarius."

What is wrong with this worldview? Experience becomes

the authority for New Agers. All truth is relative, there are no objective truths. Simple logic will demonstrate the fallacy of that statement. If someone says that all truth is relative and there is no objective truth, that belief itself becomes an absolute.

Followers of New Age philosophy do not believe in the God of the Bible. They believe God is an impersonal energy force. Both Judaism and Christianity reject this essentially Hindu concept and affirm an unshakable monotheism—a personal, benevolent, and loving Deity who is immanent within his creation and yet transcends it by infinity because he is its Creator.[6] "So we know and believe the love God has for us. God is love, and he who abides in love abides in God, and God abides in him" (1 Jn 4:16).

New Agers will admit that Jesus Christ is God, but he is no more God than anyone else. The difference between Jesus and other people is that Jesus realized and demonstrated the divine (Christ) potential that everyone has.[7] For New Agers the "Christ" is a divine principle, a "Christ consciousness" attainable by all people. "Christ is not God, he is not coming as God. He is an embodiment of an aspect of God, the love aspect of God. He is the embodied soul of all creation. He embodies the energy which is a consciousness aspect of the Being we call God."[8]

New Agers teach Christ is an energy force. "What is the Christ? Within all life there exists a quality, an energy, which has as its basic characteristic irresistible growth, irresistible and inevitable expression of divinity. It is a quality which says that whatever form I am enclosed in, I will not be held a prisoner by that form, but I will transform it into a greater form. I will use all life, all experiences as stepping stones to greater revelations of divinity. The Christ is the basic evolutionary force within creation."[9]

This energy force is called a Christ-consciousness. "The true birth of the Christ was not the birth of Jesus. Jesus was an individual who himself had to recapitulate certain stages. He built upon the pattern that Buddha had established....

He himself had to become awakened. He had to, in his consciousness, touch this Christ pattern."[10]

Jesus Christ in New Age teachings has been made an ordinary human being who had possession of an evolutionary force. He is a teacher, just like Hercules, Hermes, Rama, Mithra, Vyassa, Sankaracharya, Krishna, and Buddha. "In the esoteric tradition, the Christ is not the name of an individual, but of an Office in a Hierarchy. The present holder of that office, the Lord Maitreya, has held it for two thousand six hundred years, and manifested [it] in Palestine through His Disciple, Jesus, by the occult method of overshadowing, the most frequent form used for the manifestation of avatars (messengers of Maitreya who give people wisdom and bring peace). He has never left the work, but for two thousand years has waited and planned for the immediate future time, training His disciples, and preparing himself for the awesome task which awaits Him."[11]

Maitreya, not Jesus, is Lord in New Age circles. Maitreya is the fifth reincarnation of Buddha. Jesus became "the Christ" only after purifying himself of bad karma through many incarnations. New Agers believe he is only one of several "masters" who serves humanity from a higher plane.[12]

Jesus Christ is not a New Age master, Maitreya, or reincarnation of Buddha. When John the Baptist sent messengers to Jesus to ask him if he was the Messiah, Jesus replied, using the messianic prophecy of Isaiah: "Go and tell John what you hear and see: the blind receive their sight and the lame walk, lepers are cleansed and the deaf hear, and the dead are raised up, and the poor have the good news preached to them. And blessed is he who takes no offense at me" (Mt 11:4-6).

Jesus Christ "reflects the glory of God and bears the very stamp of his nature, upholding the universe by his word of power.... he sat down at the right hand of the Majesty on high" (Heb 1:3). Thomas proclaims Jesus to be "my Lord and my God" (Jn 20:28). Jesus himself proclaims: "I am the way, and the truth, and the life; no one comes to the Father, but by me" (Jn 14:6). St. Paul in the letter to the Galatians cautions:

"I am astonished that you are so quickly deserting him who called you in the grace of Christ and turning to a different gospel—not that there is another gospel, but there are some who trouble you and want to pervert the gospel of Christ. *But even if we, or an angel from heaven, should preach to you a gospel contrary to that which we preached to you, let him be accursed. As we have said before, so now I say again, If any one is preaching to you a gospel contrary to that which you received, let him be accursed.*" Gal 1:6-9, emphasis mine

REINCARNATION: SAVING ONESELF

The New Age Movement contradicts the gospel that Paul preached. No New Age teacher will accept Jesus Christ as the one and only Son of God sacrificed by his loving Father to save humanity from death resulting from sin. Rather, integral to NAM is the belief in reincarnation—that one's soul lives a succession of lives, gradually evolving into a perfect state, usually reached when a person becomes one with the infinite and impersonal God.[13] It is hoped that each new reincarnation gives the soul a moral and spiritual advantage over the previous life.

The purpose of reincarnation is to atone for wrongs that a person has done. In the Christian context, these wrongs are called sins. In reincarnation the persons themselves, through the choices they make in their lives, attain salvation and have no need for a personal savior.

No evidence of reincarnation is recorded in the Old or New Testament. Gnostics of the first century had faith in reincarnation, but the belief was condemned by the early church. The letter to the Hebrews asserts: "For Christ has entered, not into a sanctuary made with hands, a copy of the true one, but into heaven itself, now to appear in the presence of God on our behalf. Nor was it to offer himself repeatedly, as the high priest enters the Holy Place yearly with blood not his own; for then he would have had to suffer repeatedly since the foundation of the world. But as it is, he has appeared once for all at the end of the age to put away sin by the sacrifice of himself. And just as it is appointed for men to die once, and after that comes judgment, so Christ having been offered once to bear the sins of many, will appear a second time, not to deal with sin but to save those who are eagerly waiting for him" (Heb 9:24-28).

According to the Bible, people die only once. They do not return to earth to work through a successive series of lifetimes until they attain nirvana (paradise). No human being achieves salvation independently. Jesus Christ takes away sins. From Jesus we receive the gift of salvation.

Intrinsic to reincarnation is the law of karma—the "debt" accumulated against a soul as a result of good or bad actions committed during one's present or past life. Having accumulated good karma, the person supposedly will be reincarnated into a more desirable life. With bad karma, the person will be reincarnated into a less desirable life. Karma tries to explain pain and suffering in the world. Why do people suffer? The answer in reincarnational theology is bad karma. Since suffering is due to bad karma, it is useless to try to help one who is suffering. The person must work alone through the bad karma that caused the suffering.

Reincarnational theology leads to relativism. Actions are neither good nor evil. For example, if a woman is raped, she must have warranted it because of her bad karma. There is no such thing as murder in the law of karma. A murdered person either unconsciously wanted it to happen or bad karma was being worked out.

New Agers speak of peace. They preach about a world of goodness. They speak about freedom from hunger, disease, and suffering. They talk about a vision of wholeness for the human race. But it is only talk. The New Age Movement, based on reincarnational theology, will never be the answer for the salvation of the world. "It cannot come to grips with the fact that, while it has been talking about doing good for mankind, tens of millions of people have starved and suffered and endured horrible persecutions under India's caste system simply because reincarnation held them in a particular caste, cycle after cycle, so that it was impossible for them ever to escape. Even today in India and in other lands, people who believe this doctrine allow their children to starve while rats and sacred cows live."[14]

Reincarnational theology says it is useless to help the poor and suffering, that as a people and nation work through their bad karma and achieve wholeness, peace will come to the world. This viewpoint is not sound historically. "India is a good case in point. One would think that a land dominated for thousands of years by a holistic worldview (the same worldview that New Agers now say science has verified) would have long ago synergistically eliminated hunger, violence, overpopulation, and the institutionalized racism of its caste system. This has not happened, of course."[15]

Christianity says an emphatic *no* to reincarnational theology and the law of karma. "Since all have sinned and fall short of the glory of God, they are justified by his grace as a gift, through the redemption which is in Christ Jesus, whom God put forward as an expiation by his blood, to be received by faith. This was to show God's righteousness, because in his divine forbearance he had passed over former sins; it was to prove at the present time that he himself is righteous and that he justifies him who has faith in Jesus" (Rom 3:23-26).

NAM is not new, but a revival of paganism. This revival includes the resurgence of goddess worship. Through ritual, celebration, and myth, NAM and neo-pagans attempt to reharmonize themselves with the Whole or the One, which many groups refer to as the goddess.[16] Neo-pagans believe that patriarchal religions are responsible for the exploitation of women and nature. They believe that people must move beyond God the Father and be nurtured by the goddess within.[17] The real issue in worship of a goddess is the transcendence of God.

It appears established that the father image lends itself more readily to the dimension of transcendence, the maternal more to immanence. Maternal images bespeak closeness, connectedness to the earth and creation, and thus more easily lend themselves to pantheism. While pantheism proclaims an immanence without transcendence, the Judeo-Christian worldview holds to an immanence that presupposes transcendence, and this is expressed and preserved in various ways in the tradition, one of which is the Fatherhood of God, enriched but not replaced by maternal images of closeness. The father image, of course, runs the risk of overemphasizing the distance between God and his people; but the prophets preferred to overcome this danger by incorporating maternal imagery into the father title than to run the risk of identifying Israel's God with the process of nature by using a maternal title. Jesus himself sought to express and convey the intimacy of God within the tradition of God's fatherhood.[18]

New Agers value "unity in diversity," but the ground for this unity is pantheism. In New Age thought so-called traditional Christianity is blocking the evolution of the human race, threatening the global unity necessary for racial survival. In a New Age world there would be no tolerance for true Christianity.[19]

CRYSTALS, COLORS, CHANNELING, AND PAST-LIFE RECALL

Early in 1987 the ABC television network aired a five-hour miniseries on Shirley MacLaine's autobiography *Out on a Limb*, in which she speaks of her experiences in channeling. Channeling is a New Age form of spiritism. In channeling people open their psyches to spirits. These spirits then communicate information to them. MacLaine and other New Agers believe that the spirit is an "ascended master," who has supposedly reached the highest level of spiritual consciousness and become a guide in the spiritual evolution of the human race.

The spirit can speak only when the psyche of one channeling has been yielded to the spirit. This can happen in a variety of ways. In clairaudient channeling the message is believed to be dictated telepathically to, and repeated by, the human messenger who remains fully conscious of his or her faculties.[20] In automatisms the spirit communicates through a physical body—for example, use of a ouija board or automatic writing. Light-trance channelors are partially conscious when they channel and can remember some of the experience. Deep or full-trance channelors have no recall but fully vacate the seat of their consciousness. Full-body or incarnational channelors vacate their whole body and the spirit entities enter the body.[21]

The merging of psyches in the channeling experience is dangerous because a person's psychological integration is broken to enable the spirit to give the message. The spirit can then take up permanent residence in the psyche of the person who is channeling.

Channeling is, in effect, seeking knowledge from the dead or a demonic spirit and is, therefore, a form of divination. A familiar spirit operates differently from one that is received through channeling, even though each wish to achieve the same end. "While trance channeling involves the spirit fully inhabiting the medium's body while the medium is absent, familiar spirits function more like counselors or inner friends who communicate invisibly with the person during an altered state of consciousness."[22]

A resurgence in channeling, then called theosophy, occurred in the late 1800s and early 1900s due to the theosophy movement. Its leaders—Helena Blavatsky, Annie Besant, and Alice Bailey—received their information through channeling.

Crystals are often worn or carried by New Agers. They believe crystals contain amazing healing and energizing powers, that they help restore and set right the flow of energy of the body and mind. The belief in crystal power originates with their use in the occult. "Crystals have a long history of usage as power objects in the practices of witches, wizards, sorcerers, alchemists, shamans, and other occultic figures.

When such power objects are applied in conjunction with occultic practices, there is sometimes the subjective experience that the crystal is assisting in some ways in manipulating occult forces."[23]

New Agers claim a crystal has an electric current flowing through it that helps heal the body, but no scientific proof substantiates the claim. Crystals have no power or light in and of themselves. A crystal's current flows only during a physical change in its structure. Constant pressure on a crystal produces no continuous current. The current produced through a physical change in its structure is minutely weak, with almost no amperage.

Anthony R. Kampf, curator of minerals and gems at the Los Angeles County Museum of Natural History, says that assigning metaphysical properties to certain minerals is shades of the Dark Ages, when there was a certain amount of mysticism associated with minerals. Scientifically speaking, the minerals have no power to do what the people say they do. Samuel Adams, a director of the Geological Society of America and head of the Department of Geology and Geological Engineering at the Colorado School of Mines states that assigning curative properties to crystals "is as close to poppycock as you can get."[24]

New Agers also believe the body and mind can be healed through the use of colors. A specific infirmity calls for a specific color treatment. The person uses color lamps or stained glass to receive the treatment from one of seven basic color rays. The seven rays represent the seven "energy centers" of the body, also called *chakras*. Followers of color therapy believe that if clothing is "energized" by these color rays, the person will be healthier and happier. Again, no scientific evidence supports the theory.

One of the foundations for the New Age belief in reincarnation is past-life recall. The four main types of past-life recall are intuitive, spontaneous, psychic, and hypnotic regression. Intuitive recall is also called *déjà vu*. It is, for example, a feeling or strong impression that one has seen the same thing before, or met someone before, even though one is seeing or meeting someone or something for the first time. Reincarnationists say this event happened in a previous life.

When someone feels that they have been somewhere before or thinks that they have met a person before, they are experiencing an attempt by the subconscious mind to relate the present experience to something in the past. For instance, a person may have seen a picture or a photograph of a particular person or place and, although they can't consciously remember seeing it, their subconscious mind relates the encounter to the photograph. This causes the person to think that they have been somewhere before or met a particular person in a previous life.[25]

Spontaneous recall occurs mostly in children who insist they have lived in a previous life. These cases have not been scientifically verified. "The majority of documented cases that seem to exhibit features of supposed past lives are explained by one of the following: 1) conscious or unconscious fraud, 2) cryptomnesia, 3) genetic memory, 4) spirit communication."[26]

Psychic recall is remembering past lives through séances, mediums, or ESP experiments. This is obtaining information through occult means. Since occult means of obtaining knowledge is prohibited in the Bible and is part of the kingdom of Satan, a person should not trust those experiences as being truthful.

Hypnotic regression is recall of past lives through hypnosis. "This is the most popular argument given to support past-life recall, but is still under suspicion by many professional hypnotists.... [In hypnosis] the person is highly susceptible to suggestions and other mental or psycho-spiritual transmissions, and therefore unreliable. Those cases that involve hypnotic regression are deriving their information from memories of the subconscious or from genuine occultic sources. Neither case is sufficient to prove that reincarnation is true."[27]

The Bible warns followers of Jesus Christ to be on guard against philosophies contrary to the gospel of Jesus Christ.

Christians must be aware that Satan can disguise himself as an angel of light (2 Cor 11:14). The letter to the Philippians teaches: "At the name of Jesus every knee should bow, in heaven and on earth and under the earth, and every tongue confess that Jesus Christ is Lord, to the glory of God the Father" (Phil 2:10-11). Followers of Jesus must remember the words of St. Paul as well: "I am astonished that you are so quickly deserting him who called you in the grace of Christ and turning to a different gospel—not that there is another gospel, but there are some who trouble you and want to pervert the gospel of Christ. *But even if we, or an angel from heaven, should preach to you a gospel contrary to that which we preached to you, let him be accursed*" (Gal 1:6-9, emphasis mine).

WICCA: GODDESS WORSHIP

Another religion that worships the goddess is Wicca, or contemporary witchcraft. It is a return to pagan nature religions. Witches believe that by attuning themselves to the goddess, they can use magic spells to achieve their desires.[28] Wicca emphasizes human ties to Mother Nature.

In April, 1974, the Council of American Witches adopted a set of principles of Wiccan belief, expressing faith in pantheism, astrology, and psychic power.[29] Wicca subscribes to tarot cards, use of a pendulum (a form of the ouija board), spiritism (channeling), scrying (crystal ball gazing), palmistry, tea-leaf reading, and numerology. For witches, God is called Ultimate Deity. This deity has two parts: the god and the goddess. The goddess is often called Mother Earth or Mother Nature.

Part of Wiccan belief is reincarnation. All in the animal kingdom have souls. A dog will reincarnate as another dog. A cat will always reincarnate as a cat. A human being will always reincarnate as a human being. Those who practice Wicca also believe in the law of karma.[30]

Magical power is the method witches use to achieve what they desire. But to be effective, it must be done properly. The most important elements in magic are timing and feeling. A third is the chant or spell. Rhythmic chanting can intensify the emotion. Most magic is performed naked, whether alone or in a group. Wiccans believe magic can be both constructive and destructive.

To become a witch in a coven, one first goes through an initiation. The traditional size of the coven is thirteen people. Witches advance in the coven heirarchy through a series of steps or degrees. The traditional covendom extends for three miles in the form of a circle. Many have books on ritual magic.

Wicca encourages spiritism and many styles of divination, uses magic spells, and is rooted in pagan beliefs (reincarnation, karma, and pantheism). The Bible prohibits all these things.

The radical feminist movement contains elements of Wiccan belief. I am not stating that equal rights are bad. Equal rights are good because all are children of God. There can be a feminism that is based on biblical principles. It is the source of the radical feminist movement that is at odds with Christianity. Some leaders in the radical feminist movement are involved in the Wiccan religion. The Wiccan religion worships a goddess. Goddess worship or use of the term mother for God is inconsistent with biblical revelation.

> The term "Father (for God)," though limited as every human image and concept is, belongs to the historical core of divine revelation. Understood in its biblical sense, *it is essential and irreplaceable as the address Jesus gave for God.* It can be complemented with a vast number of metaphors, including the feminine. But the Church's public worship, in which the law of praying reflects the law of faith, cannot abandon it without dismantling the heart of Jesus' revelation.[31]

CABALA: TWISTING SCRIPTURE

At a retreat for priests in late 1990, a number of us were talking about things going on in our parishes. One mentioned that a couple of his parishioners were telling him about the great benefits of cabalas (also frequently spelled kabbalahs). He did not understand all the implications of cabala, but something did not seem right to him. He could not reconcile cabala with the New Testament.

Cabala or kabbalah is a secret doctrine. It has its roots in the ancient Jewish religion. It relies on "personal revelations." While orthodox Judaism opposes cabala, some branches of Judaism accept some of its precepts. Those who practice cabala believe that salvation is achieved through a special "esoteric" knowledge.

Cabala is a philosophical and theosophical system that was developed to answer questions about the nature of God and the universe, the destiny of the human race, and how to achieve it. Cabalists do not accept the standard translation of the Bible. They believe that the Pentateuch in Christian Bibles is not the original Hebrew text. They believe the Essenes changed it, using symbolic imagery.[32]

In cabala, God is an impersonal energy source. He is everywhere. In cabala, a person is not a creature. Rather, through secret knowledge, a person can achieve divinity and is the agent of his or her own salvation. Cabalists see no need for a personal savior.

There are some Christians who have accepted principles of cabala in their beliefs. For a Christian cabalist, God is a unity of persons, but God is not the Father, Son, and Holy Spirit that is revealed in the Bible. Christian cabalists claim that the Christian God is a misconception—that the deity manifests simultaneously as mother and father and thus begets the son. Therefore their trinity is father, mother, and son.[33] Jesus is not the Son of God; he is a master cabalist.

According to cabala, God had three motives for creating the universe. The first was to make manifest his three basic attributes: mercy, justice, and compassion. The second was to benefit the human race and bestow upon them his infinite light. As people remove the evil spirit that is incarnate in them they receive the light as a reward for their effort.[34] The third motive was to reveal his absolute unity.

Cabalists believe there are two planes of existence, the astral world and the material world (the earth). To effect a change on earth, a change must first take place in the astral world, which in turn filters down to earth. This change is accomplished through the use of magic formulas.

Cabalists also believe in reincarnation, that people have specific tasks to accomplish in their lives and if they do not fulfill them, they will be reincarnated.[35] Cabalists also believe in soul mates: "According to the Kabbalah, souls are androgynous in their original state; that is, they are bisexual in nature. When they descend to the material world, they separate into male and female and inhabit different bodies. If, during their mortal lives, the two halves of the soul meet, a great attachment develops between them, and thus it is said that through their marriage, or union, they become again conjoined."[36]

THE ENNEAGRAM: OFFSHOOT OF ISLAM

The enneagram has become a popular method for discovering the self. Many workshops have been given that encourage finding a person's enneagram personality type. While some have been very enthusiastic about this tool of self discovery, I believe that it is prudent to examine the assumptions and philosophical foundations of the enneagram before embracing its theories and practices.

The book *The Enneagram* states that the enneagram originated in Afghanistan about two thousand years ago,[37] but historians are divided about the exact date of origin. Fr. Mitch Pacwa, S.J., professor of Scripture and Hebrew at Loyola University in Chicago, states that the enneagram in its present form is only thirty years old.[38]

George Gurdjieff and Oscar Ichazzo are responsible for the enneagram in its usage today. It is important to examine their background to see if there are occult roots to the enneagram. Both men traveled extensively searching for occult knowledge.

George Gurdjieff learned the enneagram symbol from the

Sarmouni and Naqshbandi sects of Sufis.[39] The Sufi were a sect of the Muslim religion.

Sufism is Islamic mysticism. It describes the rules of life and the doctrines of Muslims "athirst for God" striving for union with him. Some people claim Muslims believe in the same God as Christians, except they don't accept Jesus Christ. However, the Islamic God is not like the Christian God. Islam rejects the biblical doctrines of the trinity and the deity of Jesus Christ.[40]

The Sufis used the enneagram for numerological divination. "They searched for the mystical meanings of the decimals .333..., .666..., and .999..., based on dividing one by three, and of .142857..., which is based on dividing one by seven and contains no multiples of three."[41] The Sufis did not attach a theory of personality to the enneagram. When Oscar Ichazzo developed his theory of personality, he incorporated this Sufi numerology into his theory.[42]

Oscar Ichazzo was greatly influenced by Gurdjieff. Ichazzo had out-of-body experiences when he was six years old. To gain control of his consciousness, he studied Oriental martial arts, Zen, Andes Indian psychedelic drugs, shamanism, yoga, hypnotism, and psychology. Ichazzo has received "revelations" from "Metratron the prince of the archangels."[43] He has a group of followers. The followers of his group are guided by "Green Qu 'Tub."

Knowing these spiritistic and occult involvements of the man who developed the enneagram personality system should signal serious concern for Christians because these occult involvements are prohibited in the Bible.

Somewhere in his spiritual search for growth, Oscar Ichazzo learned about the numerological divination of the enneagram. In 1960 he developed a system of nine personality types to correspond to the nine points on the symbol.[44] The symbol of the enneagram may date back to the ancient Sufis, but the personality theory of the enneagram is at most only thirty years old. A disciple of Ichazzo's, Claudio Naranjo, placed the enneagram into the context of psychological concepts, like Freud's defense mechanisms.

As one looks at the personality theory of the enneagram, one needs to ask some serious questions. The enneagram is a theory of personality. Has it been tested scientifically? Since psychology is a science, it is guided by a scientific method of testing. A theory is a set of statements a person uses to understand, predict, and control behavior. Hypotheses are statements about a theory. These statements are subjected to a gathering of data. In examination of the data a person asks, "Does the data support the hypothesis? Does the data support the theory?" The enneagram has not been subjected to the scientific method of testing.

How do we know that there are only nine personality types? The Myers-Briggs theory of personality typing states that there are at least sixteen personality types. The Myers-Briggs personality typing has been scientifically tested. The enneagram has not. Furthermore, how do we know that Ichazzo's nine personality types are the correct types? Can this be proven empirically? The enneagram's personality theory must be verified scientifically, otherwise it has no authority except the personal experience of those who give and take the workshops.

The enneagram view of personality postulates that each person is born with a purity of essence.[45] This means that when someone is born, he or she is a pure being, free from taint, spotless. A newborn, in the enneagram view, *has no need for redemption.* This is contrary to the scriptural view of a human being. Acts 4:11-12 declares: "This [Jesus] is the stone which was rejected by you builders, but which has become the head of the corner. And there is salvation in no one else, for there is no other name under heaven given among men by which we must be saved." Humanity needs a Redeemer. That Redeemer is Jesus Christ. It is through him that people are justified (Rom 5:12-19).

The idea of "purity of essence" denies belief in original sin. "The Council of Trent defined a real inward original sin in all (except Mary), caused by Adam's sin, [which] is effaced justification, and does not consist in concupiscence, since this persists in the justified, but in the lack of original righteousness and holiness."[46] If newborns have a purity of essence, they do not need Christ to die to redeem them. The fact is, one is born in sin (Rom 5:12-19; 1 Cor 15:21).

Ichazzo states that in order to achieve the purity of essence a person must attain a pre-ego state. Remove the ego, and a person achieves this purity of essence. The ego is the "I." The ego is the rational, realistic part of our personality. The ego permits a person to interact in the world. It is an integral part of the human personality. Yet Ichazzo says that a person must remove the ego. No reputable school of psychology supports his theories about the ego.

Fr. Pacwa states some reservations about the use of the enneagram:

> I know enough about the scientific method to know that you can't say a theory is false until it has been thoroughly tested. But as a priest and pastor, I can draw these conclusions: the enneagram personality theory is steeped in the occult. It has no scientific evidence to support its claims of validity. People who get heavily involved with it risk being diverted from the central aspects of their Christian faith.... St. Paul instructs us to "test everything; hold fast to that which is good; abstain from every form of evil" (1 Thes 5:21-22). When we test the enneagram we should use the gospel of Jesus Christ as our norm; we do not use the enneagram to test the truth of the gospel. The enneagram does not bestow eternal life. Jesus Christ our Lord does.[47]

I believe that it is wise to heed Fr. Pacwa's observations about the enneagram.

"For the word of God is living and active, sharper than any two-edged sword, piercing to the division of soul and spirit, of joints and marrow, and discerning the thoughts and intentions of the heart" (Heb 4:12). God's Word shows that the foundations of the enneagram are fraudulent. *A sound tree cannot bear evil fruit, nor can a bad tree bear good fruit*" (Mt 7:18).

A person needs to be careful when using any psychological theories in the spiritual life. Sometimes it is easy to lose perspective.

Whenever one evaluates a theory about human character, one needs to remember that wholeness is different from holiness. Wholeness refers to psychological health, and holiness to spiritual health. It is possible to have mental problems and, simultaneously, be holy. It is also possible to be mentally whole but not be holy.

Psychological adjustment and spiritual development *are different.* Psychological adjustment is a dynamic, ongoing process in which the individual seeks to make productive use of his or her abilities and at the same time fulfill personal needs adequately.

Spiritual development is built on divine grace. God is not a psychologist. He will choose people to grow in his life on his terms. Spiritual development is based upon a person's willingness to respond to God. On the other hand, a person's ability to achieve psychological adjustment is determined early in life by environment and circumstances. Throughout human history, God has been calling people who might, from the psychological viewpoint, be unlikely candidates for his mission. Remember—"many canonized saints struggled throughout life with scars and pathologies from childhood."[48] They may have had psychological problems, but they are saints.

While psychological adjustment can be an aid to growth in holiness, psychology also can hinder growth in holiness. Some schools of psychology, especially the Rogerian school, have had damaging effects on religious commitment in the church.

In order to avoid a direct confrontation with the Gospel, those who think of themselves as practicing Christians, when faced with a conflict between self-fulfillment and the higher order of Christian values, will generally adopt the rationalization: "I can't do it." It sounds better than saying,

"I won't do it." And since psychology has revealed many areas of real but relative psychological impossibility, the rationalization is a comfortable and handy one.[49]

Psychology can be a help to a person's spiritual development only when it is properly and cautiously used. The Christian must always remember that the primary goal of life is to attain holiness. The Lord said: "You shall be holy, for I am holy" (1 Pt 1:16). God did not say: "Be whole, for I am whole." He did not say: "Return to your purity of essence." If a person spent as much time meditating on God's Word in Scripture and the presence of Jesus in the Eucharist as they spent on "toys" like the enneagram, they would be much better off.

Tommy Sullivan, a sensitive fourteen-year-old Roman Catholic, was entangled in something sinister. His favorite rock group was Suicidal Tendencies. Posters of Ozzie Osbourne were on his bedroom wall. In his *Book of Shadows* Tommy wrote: "To the greatest of demons. I would like to make an exchange with you. If you will give me the most extreme of all magical powers, I will kill many Christian followers. Exactly twenty years from this day, I promise I will commit suicide. I will tempt teenagers on earth to have sex, [commit] incest, do drugs, and worship you. I believe that evil will once again rise and conquer the love of God." Did Tommy keep his chilling promises? His story is in the next chapter.

EIGHT

Satanism

TOMMY SPENT A LOT OF TIME playing Dungeons and Dragons and listening to heavy metal music. He told his friends about a dream in which Satan told him to preach satanism to other kids and then kill everyone in his family. On January 9, 1988, Tommy headed downstairs to watch *Friday the 13th* on the VCR. At 10:30 that night his father heard the smoke alarm go off and he called the police.

When the authorities arrived, they found the house splattered with blood. Tommy's mother was discovered with her throat slit and her body slashed with dozens of knife thrusts. Tommy had tried to gouge out her eyes, and also partially severed her hands. The next day officers found Tommy buried in a snowdrift. His wrists were cut and his throat slashed from ear to ear. Beside him lay the knife he had used to kill his mother and end his own life. Police pointed to his fascination with Satan as the primary influence on him to kill.[1]

Two teenagers on Long Island—Ricky Kasso, seventeen, and Jimmy Troiano, eighteen—allegedly killed Gary Lauwers, seventeen, a high school dropout, in a self-styled satanic rite. As early as the seventh grade, Ricky had engaged in digging up graves and writing lists of "the dignitaries of hell." Drugs dominated his social life. Most of Ricky's and Jimmy's friends seemed interested in séances and rituals designed to call up the devil.[2]

In Tampa, Florida, Jonathan Cantero, nineteen, was sentenced to life in prison for stabbing his mother, Patricia Ann, forty times in the chest, stomach, and back. Jonathan also slit her throat and almost severed her left hand as he recited over her body a prayer in honor of Satan. Jonathan was a self-styled satanist. He got his information from books on the occult. His murder prayer was taken from one such book: "Lord Satan, thou knowest I have stricken this woman from the earth, I have slain the womb from which I was born. I have ended her reign of desecration of my mind; she is no longer of me, but only a simple serpent on a lower plane."³

In October, 1986, an Oklahoma jury convicted Sean Sellers, seventeen, on three counts of murder: for killing his mother, his stepfather, and a convenience store clerk. Sean was an avid Dungeons and Dragons player. He kept a copy of *The Satanic Bible* in his high school locker. "In a diary which Sellers calls his 'book of shadows,' he had written, 'In the name of Satan, the ruler of the earth, and the King of the world, I command the forces of darkness to bestow their infernal power upon me.' Information presented during the trial mentioned such details of satanic doctrine as this 'book of shadows,' blood pacts with the devil, 'a code of silence,' involvement with... inverted pentagrams, high priests, recruiters, heavy metal rock music, and horror videos."⁴ In prison Sean converted to Christianity. He now tries to warn other teenagers of the dangers of satanism.

In April, 1989, Mexican federal police discovered fifteen bodies on a ranch outside of Matamoros, Mexico. The discovery came after a month of searching for Mark Kilroy, a student at the University of Texas who had disappeared during spring break. The leaders of the Matamoros group believed that they would be free from being discovered because of the ritual black magic that had been performed. Fifteen ritually-murdered people had been sacrificed in their black magic rituals. The exhumation of the bodies was particularly gruesome. Many of the officers got physically sick when they saw what had been done to the victims.⁵

These five stories have one thing in common: the perpetrators of the horrendous acts they describe were involved in some type of satanism. It is very difficult to believe that people, especially teenagers, could do such things. How did they gain their knowledge about these rituals? The history of satanism provides the answer.

Satanism and witchcraft are entangled in Western culture. Satanism involves a vow of reverence and obedience to Satan, sealed with a contract.

Satanism, in the sense of dedication to the perverse, of hostility against God and government, began in the eighteenth century in the ferment that led to the French Revolution.[6] The Black Mass, discussed later in this chapter, began in France after the middle of the seventeenth century. In it renegade priests slashed newborn babies to death over the naked bodies of young women which served as the altars for these sacrileges. Members of the French nobility paid for and attended these Masses.

"The Black Mass began late in the seventeenth century. Wanting to guarantee good fortunes for themselves, and full of the thrill of hidden blasphemy and sexual indulgence, Louis XIV's nobles—chiefly women—hired fifty or sixty renegade Catholic priests to conduct these 'special' Masses, based on the earlier (and orthodox) Masses of intention, in which a believer petitioned God for a special favor. These people were seeking power for their worldly and other worldly desires. The Black Mass was purely an invention of this period."[7]

Fr. Guidbourg recounts a Mass in which a woman stretched out on a bed, her legs and head hanging down, a napkin with a cross on it over her breast, and a chalice resting on her belly. Guidbourg cut a child's throat with a knife, drew out the blood, and poured it in a chalice. The child's body was kept to make magic powders. This was done on behalf of a great lady of the court during the reign of Louis XIV.[8]

The forerunner of contemporary satanism originated in the nineteenth century. Eliphas Levi of France romanticized magic and witchcraft. Stressing magic as a means to power, he emphasized sex and drug abuse. In the 1840s a movement began that resulted in "the Church of Carmel," led by a defrocked priest and an ex-nun.[9]

THE MAGICK OF ALEISTER CROWLEY

One of the persons responsible for the modern version of satanism is Aleister Crowley, who bridged the Black Mass of the late seventeenth century with satanism in America today. Crowley was born on October 12, 1875. His father traveled the English countryside preaching the Christian doctrines of a strict fundamentalist group, the Plymouth Brethren. As a teenager, Crowley believed he was the beast of Revelation,[10] whose mission in life was to destroy Christianity and replace it with thelema, which is ritual magic based on the Greek word for "will."

In 1898 Crowley joined the Hermetic Order of the Golden Dawn, in which he learned how to consecrate talismans, set up magic circles, and travel astrally. It was in this order that he began his studies of the ancient system of cabala covered in the last chapter, building his own system of magic largely upon it. After he was expelled from the Hermetic Order of the Golden Dawn he began a secret society in Great Britain, which he named the Order of the Silver Star.

When Crowley was twenty-eight, he visited Cairo, Egypt. There a spirit appeared to him, which he referred to as his holy guardian angel, Aiwaz.[11] Aiwaz helped Crowley formulate his theories and practice what he called "magick."

Crowley believed that any change can be effected by using the proper force. The foundation of this premise was his belief that the universe was interconnected and perfectly balanced. This is also a premise of theosophy, which Crowley studied. Crowley believed that people should subjugate the whole universe of which they are conscious to their individual wills. In this pursuit a person is free to use any force available. He stated that: "Every man has a right to fulfill his own will without being afraid that it may interfere with that of others; for if he is in his proper place, it is the fault of others if they interfere with him."[12]

The primary thrust of Crowley's belief system can be summed up in the phrase: "Do what thou wilt shall be the whole of the Law."[13] Crowley believed that people should assert themselves as individually absolute, and should use every means available to obtain what they desire. Crowley declared that every magician should study cabala because its magic is based on the balance of the universe.

Also in accord with the teachings of theosophy and eastern philosophy, Crowley believed in reincarnation and the law of karma. He said that he had gone through many incarnations of almost uncompensated wretchedness, anguish, and humiliation to accomplish his work.[14]

Crowley believed that the true magician was all-powerful, but if the rituals were not performed perfectly, the result would be disastrous. Performing the wrong action in a ritual was to be avoided at all cost, even if it meant the death of an assistant. Crowley himself killed an aide who disobeyed his commands during one of his rituals.[15]

Crowley also encouraged magicians to use divination. He described many types of divination (astrology, geomancy, tarot cards, cabala, and the I Ching). He encouraged magicians to master several methods using one or the other as the purpose of the moment dictated. "He should make a point of organizing a staff of such spirits to suit various occasions. These should be 'familiar' spirits, in the strict sense; members of his family. He should deal with them constantly, avoiding whimsical or capricious changes.... Care must be taken to employ none but spirits who are fit for the purpose, not only by reason of their capacity to supply information, but for their sympathy with the personality of the magician."[16]

In the practice of astral projection, Crowley told magicians to inhabit other organisms. He says that magicians can drive out the magical being of the organism and take possession of that organism.[17]

In his theories and practice of magick, Crowley transgressed all the commandments God has given his people in the Bible. The most heinous transgression is his belief that the blood sacrifice of a human being is the most powerful method of magic to obtain what a person is seeking. Blood is not just a symbol of life, it *is* life. According to magicians, any living being is a storehouse of energy varying in quantity, according to the size and health of the being; and in quality, according to the being's mental and moral character. They also believe that at the moment of death the human or animal energy is liberated for the purpose of the magic act. "For the highest spiritual working one must accordingly choose that victim which contains the greatest and purest force. *A male child of perfect innocence is the most satisfactory and suitable victim....* For nearly all purposes human sacrifice is the best"[18] (emphasis mine).

If it is not possible to perform a human sacrifice, then an animal sacrifice is to be substituted. The animal must be warm-blooded, in perfect health, and not too large, because of the amount of energy that will be dissipated in the ceremony.[19]

Blood sacrifice has been performed throughout human history. The Canaanites of the Middle East and the Mezo-American Aztecs offered human victims in propitiatory rites. Deuteronomy 18:10 states: "There shall not be found among you any one who burns his son or daughter as an offering." The tradition of human sacrifice also was found among ancient Greeks, Hindus, and Druids.[20] The primary function of human sacrifice was to atone for the wrongs of an entire group. Another purpose was to appease the gods after a natural disaster. Sometimes a sacrifice was offered to ensure a good harvest or continued blessings. Human sacrifice is not a thing of the past. Through the writings of people like Aleister Crowley, some misguided people believe that it is okay to perform a human sacrifice to obtain the thing they desire.

Through Aleister Crowley and his writings, satanism blossomed in England in the 1920s and 1930s. Crowley also spent some time in Italy, from which he was expelled because Italian authorities accused his followers of sacrificing infants in occult ceremonies. In the United States the press called him the "wickedest man in the world." How did Crowley, the all-powerful magician who immersed himself in the darkest areas of the occult for power and wealth, end up? A drug fiend. A blithering idiot. A heroin addict. Toward the end of his life Crowley was unable to speak coherently. He died poverty-stricken in 1947.

ANTON LAVEY: AN AMERICAN CROWLEY

Anton LaVey did for satanism in America what Crowley did for satanism in England. Anton LaVey's *Satanic Bible* draws heavily on Aleister Crowley's writings. LaVey was born to gypsy parents in Transylvania. He grew up with many legends of vampires and witches. When he was fifteen years old he became involved in the occult. Many self-styled satanists base their rituals on his books. Like Crowley, LaVey believed his mission was to destroy Christianity. His writings are the antithesis of Christianity. Indulgence is his golden rule. This is expressed in his nine satanic statements:

1. Satan represents indulgence, instead of abstinence!
2. Satan represents vital existence, instead of spiritual pipe dreams!
3. Satan represents undefiled wisdom, instead of hypocritical self-deceit!
4. Satan represents kindness to those who deserve it, instead of love wasted on ingrates!
5. Satan represents vengeance, instead of turning the other cheek!
6. Satan represents responsibility to the responsible, instead of concern for psychic vampires!

7. Satan represents man as just another animal, sometimes better, more often worse than those that walk on all fours, who, because of his "divine spiritual and intellectual development," has become the most vicious animal of all!
8. Satan represents all of the so-called sins, as they all lead to physical, mental, or emotional gratification!
9. Satan has been the best friend the Church has ever had, as he has kept it in business all these years![21]

Like Crowley, LaVey understands blood to be the energy force of life. He believes that the force is released in the death throes of the living person or creature. Even though LaVey states that no Satanist should sacrifice a human being, his writings support a purpose for human sacrifice. "The only time a Satanist would perform a human sacrifice would be if it were to serve a two-fold purpose; that being to release the magician's wrath in the throwing of a curse, and more important, to dispose of a totally obnoxious and deserving individual.... When a person, by his reprehensible behavior, practically cries out to be destroyed, it is truly your moral obligation to indulge them in their wish."[22]

LaVey and the Satanic church he began in 1966 are not significantly threatening compared to hard-core satanic cults. But his writings are. Most teenagers who have become involved in satanic rituals either began with reading his books or have read them in their continuing study of the occult. The writings of LaVey and Crowley have paved the way for the present occult phenomena.

Satanism is a system of belief incorporating four ideas:

1. Continuing demonic rebellion against God and anything godly,
2. Man as an expendable pawn in that spiritual battle,
3. Denial that the death and resurrection of Christ—God in a body—foiled the satanic plan to spite God by drag-

ging mankind into the Hell prepared for Satan and his angels, and

4. The ultimate banishment of Satan to what he chose—a place or dimension completely removed from anything having to do with God.[23]

LEVELS OF SATANISM

In the first of the five levels of satanism are those involved in divination and mild forms of traditional witchcraft or sorcery. Also included in this group are those involved in any type of spiritism (or as it is called in today, channeling).

In the second level are teenage dabblers whose lives are consumed in fantasy role-playing games like Dungeons and Dragons, suggestive heavy metal music, drugs, and séances. They have usually read *The Satanic Bible* and *Satanic Rituals* and may even have tried to perform a couple of satanic rituals.

In the third are the self-styled satanic groups or covens, who pattern their belief system on those of Aleister Crowley, Anton LaVey, and other occult authors. Many people come into contact with these groups through drug and sex parties. Teenagers are recruited by adult satanists at these gatherings. Each group shapes its teachings and ceremonies to its common interest, which makes it "self-styled" in the first place.[24]

In the fourth level are the "public religious" satanists, or those in the Church of Satan or the Temple of Set. The Church of Satan carefully screens those who wish to join. The central rite of religious satanism is the Black Mass. This level is responsible for the dissemination of the occult writings which teenagers are reading.

Fifth and last are hard-core satanists. These people have always been present throughout the world. They practice satanic ritual sacrifice, including that of humans. Many of these cults are underground. It is very difficult to substa their existence.

Belonging to this level of satanism are secret groups that are *multigenerational.* They perform bizarre rituals and are alleged to practice child sexual abuse, renting their children to others for drugs, animal sacrifice, and human sacrifice, including family members.

Dr. James G. Friesen shares the story of Fran in his book *Uncovering the Mystery of M.P.D.* (Remember that every account of alleged abuse must be carefully examined and to be fully objective needs corraborating evidence.) The following is an edited version of her story due to its graphic nature:

"I started in therapy thinking it was just incest with my father. I was sitting in group therapy about eighteen months ago, and someone mentioned something about Satan. All of a sudden I heard this voice—it was demonic. It said, 'I wish she'd shut up talking about Satan!' That is not like me at all. I had become really attuned to my own spiritual life, and that was not like me at all.

"I didn't know I had satanism in my background. (Then) I had my first flashback. It was just very, very vivid. All of a sudden I was in a barn and there were all these people, and they were chanting, and it was really, really frightening. It was so real, I immediately called my therapist. I knew what it was. When the person in group said something about Satan, it sparked my memory.

"Almost immediately after that I had this in-depth flashback of my father killing my cat, and of me having a baby and sacrificing the baby, and about being raped by the high priest, and having the demon presence entering the room. I thought that all took place when I was about seventeen—I got all those memories mixed up at first. I thought that my parents had gotten into satanism just before I left home, and this was what they finally evolved to. Little did I realize that there were twelve years of satanism going back down the scale. I thought, 'That is it—they finally got evil enough to get into satanism, and I left home.' That was not the truth. My father had brought me into satanism at the age of six. At first I remembered being almost eighteen, and then I would see myself being seventeen, and then sixteen, and all the way back to six."[25]

In her story, Fran goes on to describe how the group forced her to participate in animal sacrifices. But that was not the worst of her experiences. She goes on to share that she became pregnant through a member of the satanic cult. She gave birth to a child that was immediately sacrificed to Satan.

Fran described in details that were remarkably vivid, the sights sounds, smells, and flavors of the ritual, including chants of worship to Satan. It's horrifying and grisly. The worst was that the baby, a perfectly beautiful human being, was disposed of; the memory of her wiped out as though she had never existed.

Fran shares, "People do not understand (or are unwilling to believe) the evil that happens in satanic worship. They do not understand how anyone would give in to sacrificing a child. If you're in the most beautiful place in the presence of Jesus, you can just feel his presence, and you're engulfed in his glory. You know, in satanism it is just the opposite of that. It is so evil, that even as you are remembering these things you can feel it. You can just feel the presence of that evil. There were times with my therapist that I just knew the enemy was trying to keep a memory from me, but we would pray and it would be broken. I can't even express it in words. The presence of evil is so strong, and the fear of death is so strong. When the presence of Satan comes into a room, it's so stifling, so controlling, that you can hardly breathe. If you can imagine that there are all these other people over here calling to Satan, trying to whip it up, calling, 'Hail Satan! Hail Satan!' and they're chanting and chanting and chanting, you know the power becomes stronger and stronger, and the force of evil is so strong!"[26]

Fran's story is not an isolated case. I am presently working with two therapists who have discovered that some of their clients believe they were ritually abused in satanic ceremonies.

COVENS IN THE UNITED STATES

One name for a satanic cult is coven. Other names used are grotto band gang or circle. It is difficult for outsiders to obtain information about their activities. In the United States there are an estimated eight thousand covens with a membership of around one hundred thousand people.[27] It is impossible, however, to know this number with certainty.

There are different degrees of involvement in a satanic coven. The following is a very general scheme of these degrees or levels. Some people will get involved in only the first or second stage or degree. A few people will advance to the highest degree. A first-degree satanist is called a neophyte. People become neophytes when they enter a satanic coven. To do this candidates must pass a test. If they pass, they are given a hooded robe in plain brown material, belted at the waist with a thin, black cord, which is a symbol of their initiation into the coven.

If they are faithful to the coven and demonstrate leadership abilities, they are given a black, hooded robe. They are now ready for the next degree. Blood is taken from the left wrist. Two drops of blood are placed on the left breast of the robe. This signifies that they are an acolyte, a second-degree satanist.

Very few go beyond the third and fourth degrees. It takes many years of intense study under an *ipsissimus*, a fifth-degree satanist, to achieve the higher degrees if involvement and power. Only those who possess outstanding ability undertake these studies.

A sixth-degree satanist is called an *adept*. These people are rare. Adepts have the power to see and converse with Satan. They have the power to command the lesser demons to do their bidding. Aleister Crowley was probably the most famous adept of this century. It is even rarer to attain the seventh degree of satanism.[28]

The top-level satanists are sometimes called the *illuminati*, pure worshipers of Satan. These people are possessed, but they are also professionals.[29] Because the illuminati have given their total will and personality over to Satan, they can appear to be totally normal. They appear as angels of light, but in reality are dedicated to darkness. Hard-core satanists wish to remain unknown. It is usual for a coven leader's identity to be kept secret for the duration of leadership. It takes fifteen covens to consecrate an area to Satan.

For satanic covens, the blood sacrifice of an innocent victim is the ultimate blasphemy and a sign of devotion to Satan. In his book *Satanism,* Bob Larson shares the story of Sarah. (This account is from a report by Mr. Larson. It must be kept in mind that he has not given substantive evidence for this report.)

"They burned my girlfriend alive while I watched. She wasn't the only one killed. Another friend of mine was forced to say 'Satan, I give my life to you now,' as they pushed him over a cliff."

Sarah was petrified. "I've never told anyone before," she confessed.

Why? Her answer was simple.

"What I saw was so inconceivable, no one would believe me!"

"How did they burn your girlfriend?" I asked.

"They tied her to a platform and lit a fire under her," she explained.

"Didn't she cry for help?" I wanted to know.

"She screamed, but no one would put out the flames. They were all wearing masks so no one could see who they were," Sarah sobbed.

"What did you do while all this was going on?"

Sarah continued, "I tried to stop them, but they held me back. They made me watch and then beat me up afterwards." ... Of the two sacrifices she had seen, one body was charred beyond recognition and the other was drowned in the sea below a cliff. No traces. No evidence.[30]

Blood sacrifice is real. It happens today.

In the beginning of this chapter I reported murders by teenagers that were sacrifices to Satan. Some teenagers become so deeply involved in satanic cults or so entwined in satanic beliefs that they commit suicide.

On January 6, 1988, popular Vermont sophomore Michelle Kimball killed herself in a suicide pact with her boyfriend. He survived. Her suicide note said that she worshiped Satan and knew her parents wouldn't understand.

In Roy City, Utah, a youth's satanic oath was found in his billfold after he died of intentional carbon monoxide poisoning. The handwritten note said: "In the name of Satan, Lucifer, Belial, and Leviathan, and all the demons, named and nameless, walkers in the velvet darkness, harken to us, O dim and shadowy things, wraith-like, twisted, half-seen creatures. Welcome a new and worthy brother."

Sixteen-year-old Steve Loyacano left a note in Colorado that said he was "caught between a hatred for this world and a thirst for blood," and that he couldn't handle it. He died of carbon monoxide poisoning in the family garage.[31]

It is important to note that in the Roy City suicide, the youth's note used the demonic names Satan, Lucifer, Belial, and Leviathan. These names are chapter headings in *The Satanic Bible*. The implication is clear: reading satanic books has an evil effect upon both teenagers and adults.

In many satanic rituals the blood is mixed with urine. This mixture is consumed by those attending, so they can share in the sacrifice. They believe they receive a special power in this "communion."

Satanic ritualized murder begins in a group with the sacrificing of small animals. As the group progresses, they sacrifice larger animals, followed by the killing of human adults, and last, by the torture and murder of innocent children. The majority of people involved in satanism do not get involved to this degree. Dr. Gregory Simpson, a Los Angeles pediatrician, after examining the ritual abuse of children and examining one dead girl's chest carved with a pentagram, declared, "The conclusion I reach is that satanic abuse of small children does exist, and it's something that needs to be dealt with by the medical community."[32]

RITUAL ABUSE: A LEGAL PROBLEM

Not only the medical community but all Christian churches need to deal with these realities. Christians must no longer keep their heads buried in the sand regarding the rise of all types of child abuse, especially abuse of a spiritual nature. Spiritual abuse is more heinous from a Christian perspective, because it tries to destroy the soul of a person. One reason people refuse to believe these atrocities are happening is that it is very difficult to convict people of such crimes in a court of law. For example, in California:

Kern County's largest criminal case ever—a child molestation investigation that involved allegations of satanism and later resulted in a $500,000 state review—ended Thursday with a burst of hugs and smiles by freed defendants who got a "deal too good to refuse."
The only two defendants in jail were released Thursday night after pleading no contest to felony charges. Charges were either dismissed or promised to be dismissed against four other defendants in the case. Gerardo Gonzales, 33, pleaded no contest to one count of molesting a 5-year-old neighborhood girl in 1984.
The Rev. Willard Lee Thomas, 34, ended nine months in jail with a plea of no contest to a charge of child endangerment and to a charge in a separate case of unlawful sexual intercourse with a 17-year-old girl.
The no-contest pleas mean that the defendants are not admitting guilt but that they are offering no defense. They have the option of denying the charges in another legal proceeding.

In exchange for those pleas, Deputy District Attorney Stephen M. Tauzer agreed to dismiss 117 charges against Gonzales, 43 charges against Thomas and 43 charges against Gonzales' wife, Cheryl.

Tauzer told *The Californian* outside of court that he also would be dismissing 133 molestation charges against Brad and Mary Nokes, ages 29 and 32, and two charges against Kathy Scott, 28.

"I don't feel good about ending the case this way," Tauzer said, "but it is ended."

Tauzer said the plea bargain was arranged because the case "was difficult if not impossible to put on."

He said he believed the initial statements by children that Gonzales, Thomas and others had molested them, but he didn't know how he could convince a jury in light of the same children making later accusations that couldn't be proved.

Those later accusations were that 80 adults molested 60 children and killed 29 babies at sex orgies inspired by devil worshiping. Among the accused were a social worker, a Kern County sheriff's deputy, and a deputy district attorney.

Tauzer added that he wanted to spare the children the trauma of having to testify. He said a psychologist recently strongly recommended against the testimony of a key 8-year-old witness in the case.[33]

Police and prosecuting attorneys are still figuring out how to handle these difficult cases. Remember, the more atrocious and fantastic an accusation, the less likely someone is to believe it. Sometimes the information about satanic ritual abuse cases mysteriously disappears before it can be used as evidence in a court.

(A person in a law enforcement department stated) the evidence was disappearing from the department as quickly as it came in. The accounts of the children were compelling, convincing and consistent, and there was no question in my mind about what had happened—a ring of SRA perpetrators had been discovered. He knew one of the investigators very well, and that man was baffled about how the evidence disappeared. My acquaintance said he surely didn't want to get involved. The evil of the perpetrators was too much for him, and he didn't want to get his family in trouble with them. He wasn't going to say anything to anybody about how the evidence, which doubtless could have convicted the perpetrators, had vanished. He had to conclude that somebody in the departmental unit was on the cult side, but he was not about to go public with it. The cover-up was very successful.[34]

Keep in mind that it is very difficult to obtain objective evidence, expecially if the alleged abuse happened during a person's childhood. Therapists must be careful not to introduce into their clients' episodes something which might not have happened. Some abuse may have taken place, maybe all the alleged accusations are truthful, but in some cases it is difficult to know what kind of abuse is being alleged.

Satanic abuse allegedly occurs. More stories of this abuse are being made public. How do people become involved in Satanic rituals?

THE LURE OF SATANIC CULTS

One way is through curiosity. Maybe a person browsing in a bookstore picks up the *Satanic Bible.* Then the person might become interested in rituals described in other occult literature. He might even try a couple of them with some friends, perhaps just for kicks.

A second way people get involved in satanic cults is through severe trauma in their lives. Jerry Johnston shares the story of Mark in *The Edge of Evil.* When Mark was five years old he was molested. Because of that he wanted to run away from reality and developed his own fantasy world. At the age of twelve he practiced hypnosis and had his first out-of-body experience. When he was seventeen he started using drugs. He continued practicing astral projection and experienced some powerful things. He had one major spirit with him called the "Overseer" who had other little spirits around him. When Mark realized who these spirits were, he got out of the occult.[35]

A third way is generational, or being born of parents who are involved in cults. Jerry Johnston shares the story of Sandee in *Style* magazine. Sandee was a product of generational satanism. Her upper-middle-class family baptized her into the cult when she was four years old. Her parents are a medical professional and an elementary school teacher. Sandee attended a religious daycare center where she recognized some of the teachers as participants in satanic ceremonies at other locations. These teachers, according to Sandee, gave drugs to the children and explained the upcoming ritual to them.

Sandee attended a public school and Presbyterian church services with her parents. Like most satanists, Sandee's parents did nothing to give themselves away. By the time Sandee was a junior in high school, she had allegedly participated in the stabbing sacrifice of two infants and witnessed several ritual homicides. She fled the area to get out of the cult. She had a choice to make. Either continue in the cult or take the chance of talking about what she had experienced.[36]

A fourth way people get involved in satanism is through recruitment. Cultists promise teenagers unlimited drugs, power, sex, wealth, and recognition. They target teenagers who have emotional problems or come from dysfunctional families. They prey on the boy or girl who has low self-esteem or is confused by religious and moral values. These teens are attracted by the promise of belonging. Cultists recruit from schools, parks, churches, Dungeons and Dragons clubs, and heavy metal concerts. The recruiters do not tell them they are satanists.

Drugs and satanism have been uniquely joined for centuries. Archaeologists note that pre-Columbian cultures forged a link between sadism, terrorism, and human sacrifice by taking drugs.[37] After a while the teenager is invited to a party where they are promised free drugs and sex. The person may then be photographed in an uncompromising position (for example, while in a drugged state in a sexual position with an animal). This photograph will be used as blackmail. At these parties a lot of heavy metal music is played. In the teenager's drugged state the music filters directly into his unconscious, possibly planting seeds for deeper involvement. In this trance-like state a person identifies with the words and rhythm of the song and internalizes them.

Teenagers get involved in satanism because they're needy. They are not maniacs. They are reaching out, looking for someone to love and understand them. They are crying out to be noticed, to feel like they are someone special. The ones who get involved are often hurt and lonely. Such was the case of Sue. Fr. Joseph Brennan tells her story:

> An 18-year-old girl who was involved in this was brought to me for counseling by a friend of hers. The girl, whom I'll call Sue, had been a prostitute in a coven for two years. She said she had sex with the male members of the coven—sometimes several of them in a short span of time—as part of a ritual designed to honor Satan.
>
> When I asked how she got involved in the cult, Sue began by telling me she had been having a lot of trouble and turmoil at home. There was much squabbling between her and her stepfather. There was no peace in the home, and certainly no love between the two of them. They were constantly at each other's throats. The stress was intense. She felt alienated, unloved, unwanted.
>
> Then along came a young man who professed to care

for her. She, in turn, cared for him. She looked upon him as a shelter in a storm. She would do anything for him. She would do anything to keep him. The young man got involved in a satanic cult—and Sue followed him without much resistance. In doing so, she felt she was proving her love for him, cementing their relationship.

The cult represented the family she no longer had. She felt a sense of acceptance and belonging there. They had given her something she really wanted and, in turn, she was asked to give them something they wanted—her body. So she became a prostitute to please other members of the coven.[38]

Sue was lucky that her friend took her to Fr. Brennan. Through counseling with him she was able to get out of the cult. Unfortunately, not everyone is able to get similarly free. Some people who wish to leave never do because they fear they will be killed by the other cult members. The satanists also threaten that they will harm or kill the family of anyone who leaves. Sometimes people are blackmailed with the threat that embarrassing or illegal activities will be made public. One member of the cult "had been warned by others in the cult that if he told anyone what had happened at the ritual meeting, he would regret it. They promised him that harm would come to him and his family, and to dramatize their serious intent they put a cat in front of him and then gouged out its eyes. He was warned that the same would happen to him if he broke the code of silence."[39]

To counter the lure of Satanic cults, parents need to keep the lines of communication open with their teenagers, provide a loving Christian home, and be alert to signs of occult involvement. Practical tips are provided for parents on this in the next chapter under the heading, "Helping Teens Stay Out of Satanism."

SATANIC RITUAL CHILD ABUSE

Children are especially loved by God. Jesus in the Gospel of Mark says: "Let the children come to me, do not hinder them; for to such belongs the kingdom of God" (Mk 10:14). Satanists abhor all that Jesus stands for. Therefore it is logical that they would have a special hatred for the innocent children whom Jesus loves. Satanic ritual child abuse is the systematic degrading, demoralizing, and reprogramming of children.

Satanic ritual child abuse involves forcing children to do something against their will that is repulsive or offensive to the normal sensibilities of decent people.[40] For example, forcing children to eat their own feces or drink their own urine, eat an animal's sexual organs, or even consume the flesh of a human corpse is repulsive and offensive to normal sensibilities. These experiences are so degrading that some youngsters never overcome them.[41]

Sometimes the child abuse is sexual. It may be so brutal that surgery is required to repair the damage. One counselee of Fr. Brennan was forced to witness the birth and death of a newborn baby, murdered as an offering to Satan.[42] For defecation rituals the children are given laxatives (for example, chocolate Ex-lax). They are then smeared with their feces and sometimes forced to eat some of them.

Cases of satanic ritual child abuse are hard to prosecute because of the difficulty of infiltrating the cults. It is alleged that many times the person who tries will be killed, driven insane, or forced to join. Another reason is because evidence pointing to the rituals is destroyed. The remains of the sacrifice are cremated by "clean-up" crews whose job is to get rid of everything afterward. If the "ritual remains" have been buried on site, these crews will dig them up a few hours after everyone has left and bury them elsewhere.

Children who survive these horrors do not speak out because they are terrified. They are told cult members will kill their parents if they say anything. They also are told that if they tell what happened a bomb planted within them will explode and kill them. To reinforce the children's fear, cultists will torture and kill an animal in front of them.

Sometimes children are forced to kill babies. The cultist will hold the child's hands on a pillow and place the pillow over the baby to suffocate it, convincing the child that he or she has participated in the murder. Children also are told that if they tell what has happened, the cultists will kidnap and sell them.

Why children? Satanists want to destroy God's favored ones. Children cannot defend themselves. They are easy to manipulate. A young child can be forced into silence readily. If a court case ever came to trial, a child is the worst possible witness for the prosecution. Destruction of the young appeases the demons and, according to Aleister Crowley, the best sacrifice is a male child. The satanic cult members also hope to indoctrinate children so that in the future they will join them.

The choice of little ones is no accident. Satanists, through ritual abuse, hope to implant an evil self-concept in the child's unconscious mind to assure that he or she will do evil and not good in the future, even if not in a satanic cult. The evil burden placed upon the child is so powerful, so pronounced, that it takes on a life of its own, becoming something like a second personality.[43]

In the *Diagnostic and Statistical Manual of Mental Disorders (DSM-III-R)*, this is called Multiple Personality Disorder (MPD). Its definition is: "The existence within the person of two or more distinct personalities or personality states (each with its own relatively enduring pattern of perceiving, relating to, and thinking about the environment and self)." Also, "At least two of these personalities or personality states recurrently take full control of the person's behavior."[44] *Only a competent professional therapist is qualified to diagnose MPD. All claims of ritual abuse must be carefully investigated.*

According to Dr. Friesen, these distinct personality states occur through a process called dissociation, a defensive response to pain. Through dissociation, the person separates from the memory of a hurtful event. For example, a child experiences the trauma of abuse, and then pretends to be a new person, or alternate personality, to whom the bad things did not happen. The child has separated from the memory, which is immediately and completely forgotten. If the dissociation is complete, the amnesia is 100 percent. There also can be partial dissociation.[45]

Four theories exist about MPD: the ability to dissociate has a biological basis; about 97 percent of MPD patients have experienced abuse at an early age; abuse is ongoing in the home; and most people who dissociate have a high ability to fantasize as well as a high level of creativity.[46]

About 25 percent of children have a dissociative ability high enough to use it for relief from persistent sexual or physical abuse.[47] For the dissociation to become a preferred coping style, the pain usually begins in the pre-school years. Dissociation had to be used often enough to become a habit.[48]

The ability to dissociate takes a very gifted person, with high intellectual and creative capabilities, who also has been severely traumatized. Here is how it works: the *trauma* plus *dissociation* equals *one alternate personality* who remembers the event (the "contaminated" alter), and other alters who are protected from knowing about the trauma ("uncontaminated" alters). The uncontaminated alters retain their talents because they do not have to carry the grief of the trauma.[49]

MPD therapy is directed toward affirming the health and strength of the uncontaminated alters and then decontaminating those with traumas. Then all the alters can be integrated and the person restored to psychological wholeness.

Satanic ritual abuse of children is responsible for some cases of MPD in adults. Studies indicate that approximately 25 percent of those with MPD in North America have been subjected to satanic ritual abuse.[50] Therapists that I have spoken with verify this fact. I myself have worked as part of a team with two such cases of satanic ritual abuse. In one, the person had thirty-five alternate personalities. The patient's family had allegedly been involved in satanism since before he was born.

Satanic ritual abuse is no longer confined to families. Of the ten pre-schools in Los Angeles that allegedly have participated in this type of abuse, only one has been closed. Of the sixty-four pre-schools in California that allegedly have been involved in this abuse, only nine have been closed.

The criminal justice system of the United States that is supposed to protect the helpless has done a poor job in this area, due to the difficulty of obtaining objective evidence. Those who commit these horrendous crimes are being allowed to perpetuate their sickness while children are physically, psychologically, and spiritually destroyed. One reason is that those in power do not want to believe the children. Why don't they? Dr. Rolan Summit, head of UCLA's school of psychology, in his report *Too Terrible to Hear*, suggests seven reasons.

First, for self protection every individual is more comfortable believing in the happiness of childhood and a just society. To admit child abuse inside the home or out, is to admit those who should protect children, don't. Parents, for example, don't want to admit their judgment was off when they selected a daycare facility. To believe in demonic stories of ritual abuse forces a reappraisal of one's trust in society.

A second reason for disbelief is that people expect any legitimate victim to complain. If a child fails to make an immediate outcry, and if a child fails to describe a conventional, recognizable sort of crime, then the burden of proof rests on the child and adults who believe the child.

Third, people don't want to believe the children because of a lack of conventional evidence. Current modes of investigation are inadequate to handle this type of crime.

Fourth, these horrific crimes against children "seem to

require criminal conviction to justify public validation." The insistence of proof beyond a reasonable doubt for an invisible and illogical crime almost guarantees suppression and repudiation. For example, examine the McMartin pre-school case. The first allegations were made in the fall of 1983. Finally, in 1989 the case came to trial. Imagine children having to recount—to relive—their bizarre stories of abuse and mind-bending pain year after year.

Fifth, the message of atrocious experiences such as satanic ritual abuse of children is unwelcome. Anyone who participates in uncovering a suspected nest of exploitation may now be accused of coaching witnesses into false accusations.

Sixth, the public doesn't really believe in satanic crime—especially ritualized child abuse. Also many parents refuse to let their abused children undergo the trauma of telling and retelling what happened. The public is basically content with not having to deal with the issue. Cases also may be suppressed by authorities—for example, a doctor, judge, or attorney who may be a silent cultist.

The final reason is that awareness of these crimes is so new. Law enforcement agencies need to develop methods of finding evidence and methods of prosecution. Investigators are hopelessly outclassed by the practitioners of these crimes.[51]

SYMPTOMS OF RITUAL ABUSE

Catherine Gould, Ph.D. and clinical psychologist, is one of the foremost therapists in counseling victims of satanic ritual child abuse. In 1986 I attended a conference at Pepperdine University where she was a guest speaker. She provided the following list of symptoms characterizing satanic ritual abuse involving pre-school age children, not usually seen in sexual abuse cases. Some professional therapists disagree with this criteria. I present Dr. Gould's criteria to you as general guidelines.

upation with urine and feces. Use of words for
nd feces that are not used at home (especially
___y words like "poopoo").
2. Discussion of feces or urine on the face or in the mouth.
Constant discussion of urine and feces at the dinner
table.
3. Urine or feces strewn or smeared in the bathroom.
4. Inability to toilet train a child because the child is afraid
(as opposed to not ready to be toilet trained or in a power
struggle with the parent). The child may reveal fears of
having to eat the feces after using the toilet.
5. Preoccupation with passing gas. Using mouth to make
gas sounds repeatedly, attempting to pass gas purposely,
wild laughter when the child or someone else passes
gas. Use of words for passing gas at home that are not
used at home.
6. Aggressive play that has a marked sadistic quality. The
child hurts others intentionally, and seems to derive
pleasure from doing so. Child destroys toys.
7. Mutilation themes predominate. Child acts out severing,
sawing off, twisting or pulling off body parts. Aggressive
words include cut, saw, slice, and chop. Taking out eyes
or removing other parts of the face and head are common themes.
8. Harming animals, or discussion of animals being hurt
or killed.
9. Preoccupation with death. Child "practices" being dead,
asks if he or she will die at age six (the satanic number),
and asks whether we eat dead people. Questions are dis-
tinguishable from normal curiosity about death by their
bizarre quality.
10. Fear that there is something foreign inside the child's
body—for example, ants, ice, or a bomb.
11. Fear of going to jail, being tied up, or caged. References
to the police coming after the child.
12. Abnormal fear of ghosts and monsters. Child's play fre-

quently involves ghosts and monsters.

13. Fear of "bad people" taking the child away, breaking into the house, killing the child or the parents, or burning the house down.

14. Child is clingy and resists being left with baby-sitters, especially overnight.

15. Child's level of emotional or behavioral disturbance seems inconsistent with the parents' level of functioning.

16. Preoccupation with the devil, magic, potions, supernatural powers, or crucifixions. Questions about these topics in families who do not believe in them or discuss them are significant.

17. Odd songs or chants by the child that are sexual or otherwise bizarre, or that have a "you better not tell" theme.

18. Numbers or letters always written backwards (as opposed to a child who sometimes or often reverses numbers or letters). This is the "devil's alphabet."

19. References to drugs, "pills," candy, mushrooms, "bad medicine," or injections that seem peculiar for a preschool age child. References to drug-like or diuretic effects.

20. Constant fatigue, illness, or flare-up of allergies. Vomiting.

21. References to people at school who are not school personnel. (This is because other adults join teachers for the abusive activities.)

22. References to "my other daddy," "my other mommy," or "my other family" (meaning "at school").

23. References to television characters as if they were real people. (This is because perpetrators take on names like "Barney Rubble," so a child's disclosures will be dismissed as television-inspired fantasies.)

24. References to people in scary costumes, especially monsters, ghosts, devils, or Dracula.

25. References to sexual activity with other children at school.

26. Discussion of being taken to people's houses or other

locations (junkyard, church, hospital, another school) that are not normal school outings for which parents have given permission.

27. References to pictures or films being taken at the school at times other than when school pictures would normally be taken. Peculiar descriptions or references to nudity, sexual acts, unusual costuming, or animal involvement when discussing photography at school.

28. Marks on child's back, unusual bruising, especially in patterns.

29. Nightmares or dreams of any of the above.[52]

Catherine Gould also provided a list of symptoms characterizing satanic ritual abuse and sexual abuse in pre-school age children:

1. Low self-esteem, feeling of being "bad." Child feels deserving of punishment.

2. Child is fearful, clingy, regresses to "baby" behavior. Child demonstrates separation anxiety.

3. Child is angry, aggressive, and acts out.

4. Child acts wild, uncontrolled, and hyperactive.

5. Child is accident prone, or deliberately hurts self.

6. Child is negativistic and resistant to authority. Child mistrusts adults.

7. Child is over-compliant to authority or overly pleasing to adults.

8. Child shows rapid mood changes.

9. Child is withdrawn, does not play, or plays in lethargic, unfocused way.

10. Child exhibits short attention span.

11. Child does not learn.

12. Child's speech is regressed and babyish. Child has delayed speech or speech disorder. Child's speech production decreases significantly.

13. Somatic complaints—stomachaches, nausea, or vomiting.
14. Nightmares or sleep disorders.
15. Child is fearful of being touched. Child fears having genital area touched.
16. Child touches genitals or masturbates excessively. Child touches or tries to insert finger in rectum.
17. Child pulls down pants, pulls up dress, or takes off clothes inappropriately.
18. Child touches others sexually or asks for sex.
19. Child is sexually provocative or seductive.
20. Child complains of vaginal or anal pain, burning when washed, or pain when urinating or defecating.
21. Semen or blood stains on child's underwear.
22. Detailed and age-inappropriate understanding of sexual behavior.
23. "Hints" about sexual activity.
24. Complaints that an adult or older child is "bothering" the child.
25. Reference to blood or urine or "white stuff" in genital area.
26. Statement that someone removed the child's clothes.
27. Statement that older child or adult exposed him or herself to the child.
28. Statement that an older child or adult touched or penetrated the child's bottom, vagina, rectum, mouth, etc.
29. Statement that child touched an older child's or adult's bottom, vagina, penis, rectum, etc.
30. Statement that the child witnessed sex acts.
31. On exam, relaxed sphincter, anal or rectal laceration or scarring; child relaxes rather than tenses rectum when touched.
32. On exam, enlargement of vaginal opening or vaginal laceration or scarring in girls. Sore penis in boys. Blood or trauma around genital area.
33. On exam, venereal disease.[53]

In targeting little children for abuse, satanic cultists become involved in pre-schools as teachers or administrators as a cover. It is difficult to distinguish a "safe" pre-school from one where abuse is being practiced. To make decisions regarding a pre-school, Dr. Gould advises the following:

1. Experience shows that so-called "open" schools are as prone to satanic ritual abuse as closed. That is, being able to walk directly into the classroom does not guarantee safety. A "watch person" alerts perpetrators that a person is arriving, and the child is quickly produced.

2. Several of the offending schools have two-way mirrors in the classrooms. These are almost never "single perpetrator" cases. Rather, from what children have revealed, the whole school seems to be involved. Therefore the ability to look into the classroom and see what is going on provides no deterrent.

3. Personnel at offending schools do not seem obviously "strange." After a child discloses abuse at the school, parents rarely think in retrospect that they should have suspected it based on the teachers' behavior. Some personnel at offending schools may even be exceptionally "solicitous" of the child's academic progress. When the child does not progress (because they are being abused) the school may recommend that they be retained an extra year.

4. The expense, prestige, religious, or educational affiliation of a pre-school seems to provide no assurance that the school is safe. Children from such schools have made extensive and detailed allegations of abuse. Similarly, children from college and university affiliated pre-schools have alleged abuse. Religiously affiliated pre-schools also have numbered among the offenders.

5. Satanic ritual abusers tend to infiltrate pre-schools in

clusters, by geographic area. For example, in the South Bay area of Los Angeles seven offending pre-schools were identified as of 1986. Also in California, as of 1986, clusters of offending schools were identified in the Newbury Park, Whittier, and Riverside areas.

6. Confronting the school with the child's allegations of abuse will produce nothing other than denials that such activity is going on. The school may submit to "investigation" by the police, which usually involves little more than "talking to" the pre-school director. Sometimes the school will threaten to sue the parents if they file a complaint.[54]

Remember that it is extremely difficult to prove the allegations that are made in cases of satanic ritual child abuse. But the situation is not hopeless. Christians are a people of hope. The surest way to protect children from the dangers of satanism and satanic ritual abuse is to have a home that is centered on prayer and open communication. When a family prays together and has open and honest dialogue there is little danger that Satan will ensnare the children of that family.

Love—your love and the love of God—can bring anyone to wholeness and healing. The one thing that satanic cultists wish to rob from children is the ability to love and be loved. Fr. Joseph Brennan consoles, "I have never seen a child brought to me for counseling who does not have this urge to love again and to be loved again."[55]

These children, the little ones of the Lord, need to be assured that they are loved very dearly. They need to be taught that they are not evil, but are good. Satanic ritual abuse is programmed to build an evil self-image into its victims. Only with love, both human and divine, and the constant assurance of the goodness of the child, will the evil bondage be broken.

THE BLACK MASS

The best known satanic ritual is the Black Mass, which originated during the reign of Louis XIV in the eighteenth century, to worship Satan. The Mass follows the format of the Catholic Mass, but the prayers are prayed backwards and praise of Satan replaces praise of God. However, many Satanists today do not use the black mass for their rituals.

If possible, a defrocked priest is the celebrant. The satanic altar is a table, about six feet long and two to three feet wide. A nude woman is placed upon the altar, her legs spread open. A pentagram is traced upon her stomach. Its five points represent earth, air, fire, water, and spirit. The candles on the altar are black and made from the fat of unbaptized babies. The "chalice" used by the satanists may be fashioned of any metal except gold. It contains a mixture of wine and the urine of a prostitute. A sword may be used in the ritual as a sign for power, or to perform a human sacrifice if there is to be one. A bell, used to begin the ritual, calls forth the powers of darkness. A baphomet or inverted cross is placed near the altar.

Satanists are sent to Catholic churches to try to obtain a host from the celebration of the Catholic Mass. The consecrated host is desecrated throughout the ceremony. If a consecrated host cannot be obtained, then a human sacrifice is performed. If there is a human sacrifice, the blood of the victim is mixed with the contents of the chalice and all present take "communion" from this mixture. After the communion the participants conclude the ritual with a sexual orgy.

Most satanic covens have feast days that are close to the calendar of feasts of the Catholic church. The activities performed depend upon the nature of the feast. The date for the celebration of a feast may change depending on the coven, but almost every coven has some type of ritual ceremony between October 29 and November 2. Fr. Joseph

Brennan in *The Kingdom of Darkness* prov[...]
chart:[56] There are many Satanic calendars.[...]
most popular ones used.

SATANIC RITUAL CALENDAR

Date	Celebration Ritual	Ritual	Age/Gender/Species
1/7	St. Winebald Day	Blood	15–33/m./human
1/17	Satanic Revels	Sexual	7–17/f.
2/2	Satanic Revels	Sexual	7–17/f.
2/25	St. Walpurgis Day	Blood	Animal
3/1	St. Eichatadt Day	Blood	Any age/m. or f.
3/20 or 21	Spring Equinox	Orgies	Any/m. or f. human or animal
4/21–26	Prep. for the Sacrifice		
4/26	Grand Climax	DaMeur	1–25/f.
6/21 or 22	Summer Solstice	Orgies	Any age/m. or f. human or animal
7/1	Demon Revels	Blood	Any age/f.
8/3	Satanic Revels	Sexual	7–17/f.
9/7	Marriage to the Beast	Sexual	Infant to 21/f.
9/21 or 22	Fall Equinox	Orgies	Any age/m. or f. human or animal
10/29–11/1	Halloween	Blood/Sexual	Any age/m. or f.
11/4	Satanic Revels	Sexual	7–17/ f.
12/21 or 22	Winter Solstice	Orgies	Any age/ m. or f., animal or human
12/24	Demon Revels	DaMeur	Any age/m. or f.

I believe that we as Christians have an obligation to pray for the victims of the rituals performed on these days. We also

n obligation to pray for the conversion of satanists who
the perpetrators of these vile acts. Catholics could attend
Mass and intercede that God will manifest his healing power to
the victims and a spirit of repentance to the perpetrators. God
equips us to combat the onslaught of the enemy. "One man of
you puts to flight a thousand, since it is the Lord your God
who fights for you"(Jos 23:10). The next chapter shows how to
move out of darkness into the light of Jesus Christ as we exercise the authority we have been given in Jesus' name.

Part Three

Freedom from Darkness

NINE

Renouncing the Occult

T HE CALL OF A FOLLOWER OF Jesus Christ is to "be holy; for I the LORD your God am holy" (Lv 19:2). Holiness is following the will of God daily and growing in his love. People have true happiness and joy only when they are living in union with their Creator. "For the kingdom of God is not food and drink but righteousness and peace and joy in the Holy Spirit" (Rom 14:17). But sometimes the striving for union with God gets misdirected. This is what happens when someone becomes involved in the occult.

Satan robs people of the joy to be found in union with God through deception, for he is the father of lies. Liar that he is, Satan promises happiness, but he cannot deliver. Those who have followed Satan will have happiness only when they leave him and commit their lives to Jesus Christ.

To be free from ties to Satan, a person must renounce the occult. Their renunciation should be spoken three times—once for each aspect of the demonic trinity. The person's *specific activity* in the occult should be a part of the renunciation.

A Christian can break this bondage through the power of the name of Jesus. Christ gave authority to those who follow him (Lk 10). Through his death and resurrection, Jesus destroyed the power of Satan, but Satan continues to wage guerrilla warfare against Christians. However, that is all he can do. He cannot win the battle. Jesus has already done that! Satan trembles when Christians use the name of Jesus. And

obey the command of Christians when they use
ne.

er is in order here. There are many approaches to
leading ose who have been involved in the occult in a
prayer of renunciation. No one approach among those who
minister is necessarily better than all the others. In this vein,
what follows is a simple prayer of renuncialtion that the Lord
has led me to use in helping people to renounce their involvement in the occult.

In the name of Jesus Christ, Son of the Living God, I renounce my involvement in (mention specific area of occult... ouija board, tarot cards, séances, Silva Mind Control,
witchcraft, etc.). Pray this prayer of renunciation three
times. If a satanic pact has been entered into, renounce the
promise you made to Satan word for word (or as close to
the actual wording as possible) three times.

I now invite you, Jesus, into my life. I give you, Jesus, my
heart, my mind, my soul, and my strength. I accept you as
my only Lord. I accept you as my only savior. I ask you,
Jesus, to send me the Holy Spirit.

I invite you, Holy Spirit, into my life. Holy Spirit, fill me
with your presence from the crown of my head to the soles
of my feet. Place within me a desire for union with God, my
Father. And I ask you, Holy Spirit, to give me the gift of
prayer.

What I provide in this chapter is only some basic information on renunciation of the occult. For a more in-depth treatment, one can read *Deliverance from Evil Spirits; A Weapon for
Spiritual Warfare* by Fr. Michael Scanlan, T.O.R., and Randall
Cirner (Ann Arbor, Michigan: Servant Publications, 1980).

Along with active renunciation of the occult, a Catholic
also should go to the Sacrament of Reconciliation to receive
the forgiveness of God and the blessing of the church.

People give part of their mind and will to Satan through
participation in the occult. These people must claim their

mind and will back for the glory of God. They m
know, beyond a shadow of a doubt, that he is not
their lives. They must now turn their lives over to
If they don't, something worse may happen to th   ....hen
the unclean spirit has gone out of a man, he passes through
waterless places seeking rest, but he finds none. Then he
says, 'I will return to my house from which I came.' And
when he comes he finds it empty, swept, and put in order.
Then he goes and brings with him seven other spirits more
evil than himself, and they enter and dwell there; and the
last state of that man becomes worse than the first. So shall it
be also with this evil generation" (Mt 12:43-45).

To stay free from harm, people who have been deeply
involved in satanism must follow the Lord. The spiritual pressure from the darkness can be great enough to disintegrate
the personality. Only the light of Jesus Christ can stop it,
bringing healing and peace.

Of course, the best medicine is preventive medicine. We
take care of ourselves by using a proper balance of nutrition,
exercise, and rest so we won't get sick. We must also take care
of our spiritual life so that we won't get spiritually sick. Growing in holiness is preventive medicine against Satan and his
deceptions. It is the work of all Christians. This is not easy. It
takes discipline. It takes hard work.

> For we are not contending against flesh and blood, but
> against the principalities, against the powers, against the
> world rulers of this present darkness, against the spiritual
> hosts of wickedness in the heavenly places. Therefore take
> the whole armor of God, that you may be able to withstand
> in the evil day, and having done all, to stand. Stand there-
> fore, having girded your loins with truth, and having put
> on the breastplate of righteousness, and having shod your
> feet with the equipment of the gospel of peace; besides all
> these, taking the shield of faith, with which you can quench
> all the flaming darts of the evil one. And take the helmet of
> salvation, and the sword of the Spirit, which is the word of

God. Pray at all times in the Spirit, with all prayer and supplication. To that end keep alert with all perseverance,
making supplication for all the saints. **Eph 6:12-18**

As one prays this Scripture he or she should reflect upon
each part of the armor. To place the belt of truth upon oneself means to live in the truth of Jesus Christ. What is that
truth? Jesus is Lord. Jesus loves me and accepts me. He gave
his life for me. Jesus forgives me all my sins.

To place the breastplate of righteousness upon oneself
means to live in the justice and truth of God. Living in the
justice of God is possible only when one is following the will
of God. This takes discipline, and resisting the desire to live
in one's own sense of righteousness.

To place the gospel of peace upon oneself as footgear is to
be the peace of Christ to all one meets. Christians are to represent the love of God to the world. Their actions and words
are to spread this love.

To take up the shield of faith to ward off the fiery darts of
Satan means to believe in the power of God's love. Satan, the
author of lies, will hurl doubts about God's love for those who
believe in him. The shield of faith blocks these doubts. The
shield of faith assists the believer in remembering God's
promises.

To place the helmet of salvation upon oneself is to protect
one's thoughts. Second Corinthians 10:5 encourages Christians to "take every thought captive to obey Christ." This is essential because the mind is the battleground and Satan wants
it. Satan wants people to choose him freely. He tries to lead
people into his kingdom of darkness through tempting
thoughts. The helmet of salvation helps the person to follow
the Lord instead. Christians must claim their minds and wills
for the glory of God. Every thought is to be purified by being
made captive to Christ.

To take up the sword of the Spirit is to read and meditate
upon the Word of God. It does no good to have a Bible in a
house unless it is read. The Bible is God's Word to his people.

They need to reflect upon it every day to grow in holiness. The Lord's people will know him when they meet him in the Scriptures and reflect upon his Word.

Along with placing the armor of God upon oneself each day, each of us should ask Jesus to cover ourselves and our families with his precious blood. Along with this covering, we should ask for the protection of the mantle of Mary, the mother of Jesus. Asking for the intercession of the angels and saints also gives protection from Satan's attacks. (See chapter six for an explanation of the Catholic devotion to the saints.)

THE ARMOR OF PRAYER AND FAITH

Growing in holiness means growing in daily prayer. A person seeking holiness should strive for a vibrant prayer life. Prayer can take many forms: praying in one's home, whether the prayers are devotional or spontaneous; listening to Christian music; reading and reflecting on the Bible, or celebrating at church services.

Sometimes it seems difficult to find the time. Fr. Michael Scanlan suggests making an appointment with God each day and writing it on the daily schedule. If a day is so programmed there is no time for prayer, the solution is simple: get up earlier.

Every morning I pray the following, which was composed by Sister Betty Igo and myself on a trip to Yugoslavia. (Part of this prayer is contained in Fr. Robert DeGrandis' book *Intergenerational Healing.*) First, imagine and feel your family and yourself under the cross, covered with his light and precious blood, then pray:

> I welcome the power of the resurrected Christ in any stronghold Satan thinks he may have in or around me, and in the name of Jesus I break any generational or personal hold of the spirits that torment me or my generations.
>
> I place upon myself the helmet of salvation, the breastplate of righteousness, the belt of truth and the shoes of

the gospel of peace. I take up the shield of faith and the sword of the spirit, the word of God.

In the name of Jesus Christ and by my authority as a Christian I bind you, Satan, and all demonic spirits on the earth, in the air, in the fire, in the water, in the atmosphere, in the netherworld, and all the satanic forces of nature. I bind you from any intercommunication or interrelationship with each other. I separate you totally and completely from each other.

(Pray three times the following paragraph:)

In the name of the Father, the Son, and the Holy Spirit I rebuke and bind any spirit not of our Lord Jesus Christ and I command it to leave my presence, possessions, and loved ones. I bind and break every satanic sacrifice, curse, hex, seal, spell, sorcery, and anything else of like nature, also any disease placed upon me or my family by any agent or brought upon us by our own mistakes or sins.

In the name of Jesus Christ I bind all spirits of the north, south, east, and west, and all other evil spirits trying to influence the personnel, functions, and property of my parish. Lord God, send your angels into these regions to draw your people to you.

Mary the Immaculate, clothe me in the light, power, and energy of your faith. Father, please assign angels and saints to assist me. I ask that my guardian angel protect me from sin. Thank you, Jesus, for being my wisdom, my justice, my sanctification, and my redemption. I surrender to the ministry of the Holy Spirit.

Glory be to the Father, and to the Son, and to the Holy Spirit. As it was in the beginning, is now, and ever shall be. Amen.

Prayer to St. Michael the Archangel:

Saint Michael the Archangel, defend us in the battle. Be our protection against the wickedness and snares of the devil. May God rebuke him, we humbly pray, and do thou,

O Prince of the Heavenly Host, by the power of God, thrust into hell Satan and all evil spirits who wander through the world for the ruin of souls. Amen.

Frequent reception of Communion and the Sacrament of Reconciliation is important in the life of a Catholic. Jesus gave the apostles the power to forgive sins in his name when he said: "If you forgive men's sins they are forgiven them; if you hold them bound they are then held bound." The power to forgive sins in the name of Jesus has been passed down through the centuries by the Sacrament of Holy Orders to the bishops and priests of today. Living in forgiveness frees one of resentments and hurts. Christians also should confess their sins daily to the Lord. An excellent method is praying Psalm 51.

The reception of Communion, also called the Eucharist, is extremely important to Catholics. The Eucharist is the Body and Blood of Jesus Christ. While it is good to ask for the protection of the blood of Christ each day, it is better to ask it during the Eucharistic celebration, when one receives the Body and Blood of Christ. Throughout its history, the Catholic church has emphasized the power of the Body and Blood of Christ. Miracles have demonstrated that the bread and wine are in fact changed into Christ's Body and Blood. The bread and wine are not merely symbols of Jesus—they become the body and blood of Christ.

In about the 700th year of Our Lord, in a monastery then named for St. Longinus, the Roman centurion who pierced the side of Christ with a lance, a priest-monk of the Order of St. Basil was celebrating the Holy Sacrifice of the Mass according to the Latin Rite. Having suffered from recurrent doubts regarding transubstantiation (the change of the bread and wine into the Body and Blood of Christ), he had just spoken the solemn words of Consecration when the host was suddenly changed into a circle of flesh, and the wine was transformed into visible blood.

Bewildered at first by the prodigy which he had witnessed, he eventually regained his composure, and while weeping joyously, he spoke to the congregation: "O fortunate witnesses, to whom the Blessed God, to confound my unbelief, has wished to reveal Himself visible to our eyes! Come, brethren, and marvel at our God, so close to us. Behold the flesh and blood of our Most Beloved Christ."

The congregation rushed to the altar, marveled at the sight, and went forth to spread the news to other townspeople who, in turn, came to the church to witness the Eucharistic miracle for themselves. The flesh remained intact, but the blood in the chalice soon divided into five pellets of unequal sizes and irregular shapes.

The Host and the five pellets were placed in a reliquary of artistic ivory. Over the years they have been in the keeping of three different religious orders. The ivory reliquary was replaced in 1713 by the one which now exhibits the two relics.

A number of these authentications have been performed throughout the centuries, but the last verification, in 1970, is the most scientifically complete. Performed under strict scientific criteria, the task was assigned to Professor Doctor Odoardo Linoli, university professor-at-large in anatomy and pathological histology, and in chemistry and clinical microscopy, head physician of the united hospitals of Arezzo. Professor Linoli availed himself of the services of Doctor Ruggero Bertelli, a professor emeritus of normal human anatomy at the University of Siena. Dr. Bertelli not only concurred with all of Professor Linoli's conclusions, but also presented an official document to that effect.

The conclusions reached by Professor Linoli were presented on March 4, 1971, in detailed medical and scientific terminology to a prestigious assembly, including ecclesiastical officials.

As a result of the histological (microscopic) studies, the

following facts were ascertained and documented: The flesh was identified as striated muscular tissue of the myocardium (heart wall) having no trace whatsoever of any materials or agents used for the preservation of flesh. Both the flesh and the sample of blood were found to be of human origin, emphatically excluding the possibility that it was from an animal species. The blood and the flesh were found to belong to the same blood type, AB. The blood of the Eucharistic miracle was found to contain the following minerals: chlorides, phosphorus, magnesium, potassium, sodium to a lesser degree, and a greater quantity of calcium proteins in the clotted blood were found to be normally fractionated, with the same percentage ratio as those found in normal fresh blood.

Professor Linoli further noted that the blood, had it been taken from a cadaver, would have altered rapidly through spoilage and decay. His findings conclusively exclude the possibility of a fraud perpetrated centuries ago. In fact, he maintained that only a hand experienced in anatomic dissection could have obtained from a hollow internal organ, the heart, such an expert cut, made tangentially—that is, a round cut, thick on the outer edges and lessening gradually and uniformly into nothingness in the central area. The doctor ended his report by stating that while the flesh and blood were conserved in receptacles not hermetically sealed, they were not damaged, although they had been exposed to the influences of physical, atmospheric, and biological agents.[1]

One who wants to follow Christ should become involved in church. Regular attendance is necessary, for the Lord tells his people, "Remember the sabbath day, to keep it holy" (Ex 20:8).

Making the sign of the cross is a powerful prayer. Through it, Satan is confronted with the reality that he has been vanquished. A crucifix can be a great weapon against Satan, because it is through the cross that people receive redemption.

Christians should incorporate praise into their prayer life. Praying in tongues can be of great assistance. This gift is often experienced by Catholic charismatics and Protestant pentecostals and is given by the Holy Spirit (1 Cor 12:10). St. Paul says, "I thank God that I speak in tongues more than you all" (1 Cor 14:18).

While praying in tongues comes from the Holy Spirit, it remains under the control of the person's will. This gift is the power of the Holy Spirit praying within the person. Praying in tongues was called jubilation in the early church.[2] Singing in tongues was a part of the liturgy of the church until the ninth century.[3] I encourage you to read *Sounds of Wonder* by Eddie Ensley for an excellent history and description of this gift, also called praying in the Spirit. Ephesians 6:18 encourages the followers of God to pray in the Spirit.

Catholics should ask for the intercession of the Blessed Virgin Mary in their daily lives. This powerful prayer can be made through praying the Rosary. Genesis 3:15 declares: "I will put enmity between you (Satan) and the woman (Mary), and between your seed and her seed; he shall bruise your head, and you shall bruise his heel." Luke 1:48 says of Mary: "all generations will call me blessed." Jesus, on the cross, gave his mother to us to be our spiritual mother. Because Mary is the mother of Jesus, she has a special place in heaven, from which she intercedes for the followers of Christ on earth.

A full prayer life includes fasting, in which one seeks the discipline of God to turn away from sin. A fast can be total (no solid food, only water) or partial. One also can fast by not eating foods he or she enjoys.

Homes should be dedicated to the Lord, thereby inviting his presence. An excellent method is the enthronement of the Sacred Heart. Religious articles and pictures in a home also remind people to center their lives on God.

Devotional prayers, such as the chaplets of St. Michael the Archangel, the Holy Spirit, the Sacred Heart, and the Divine Mercy, protect people from demonic influence.

CHAPLET OF ST. MICHAEL THE ARCHANGEL

O God come to my assistance.
O Lord, Make haste to help me.
Glory be to the Father, etc.

First Salutation: One Our Father and three Hail Marys in honor of the first Choir of Angels. By the intercession of St. Michael and the celestial choir of seraphim, may the Lord make us worthy to burn with the fire of perfect charity. Amen.

Second Salutation: One Our Father and three Hail Marys in honor of the second choir of angels. By the intercession of St. Michael and the celestial choir of cherubim, may the Lord vouchsafe to grant us grace to leave the ways of wickedness and run in the paths of Christian perfection. Amen.

Third Salutation: One Our Father and three Hail Marys in honor of the third choir of angels. By the intercession of St. Michael and the celestial choir of thrones, may the Lord infuse into our hearts a true and sincere spirit of humility. Amen.

Fourth Salutation: One Our Father and three Hail Marys in honor of the fourth choir of angels. By the intercession of St. Michael and the celestial choir of dominion, may the Lord give us grace to govern our senses and subdue our unruly passions. Amen.

Fifth Salutation: One Our Father and three Hail Marys in honor of the fifth choir of angels. By the intercession of St. Michael and the celestial choir of powers, may the Lord vouchsafe to protect our souls against the snares and temptation of the devil. Amen.

Sixth Salutation: One Our Father and three Hail Marys in honor of the sixth choir of angels. By the intercession of St. Michael and the celestial choir of virtues, may the Lord preserve us from evil, and suffer us not to fall into temptation. Amen.

Seventh Salutation: One Our Father and three Hail Marys in honor of the seventh choir of angels. By the intercession of St. Michael and the celestial choir of principalities, may God fill our souls with a true spirit of obedience. Amen.

Eighth Salutation: One Our Father and three Hail Marys in honor of the eighth choir of angels. By the intercession of St. Michael and the celestial choir of archangels, may the Lord give us perseverance in faith and in all good works, in order that we gain the glory of paradise. Amen.

Ninth Salutation: One Our Father and three Hail Marys in honor of the ninth choir of angels. By the intercession of St. Michael and the celestial choir of angels, may the Lord grant us to be protected by their mortal life and conducted hereafter to eternal glory. Amen.

At the end say four Our Fathers on the four large beads nearest the medal—the first in honor of St. Michael; the second, St. Gabriel; the third, St. Raphael, and the fourth, our guardian angel.

Then say the following invocation:

O glorious prince St. Michael, chief and commander of the heavenly hosts, guardian of souls, vanquisher of rebel spirits, servant in the house of the divine king, and our admirable conductor, thou who dost shine with excellence and superhuman virtue, vouchsafe to deliver us from evil, who turn to thee with confidence, and enable us by thy gracious protection to serve God more and more faithfully every day. Pray for us, O glorious St. Michael, prince of the church of Jesus Christ, that we may be made worthy of his promises.

Almighty and everlasting God, who by a prodigy of goodness and a merciful desire for the salvation of all men, hast appointed the most glorious archangel St. Michael, prince of thy church, make us worthy, we beseech thee, to be delivered by his powerful protection from all our enemies, that none of them may harass us at the hour of death, but that we may be conducted by him into the august presence of thy divine majesty. This we beg through the merits of Jesus Christ our Lord. Amen.

CHAPLET OF THE HOLY SPIRIT

This chaplet consists of five groups of seven beads each. Before and after each group are two large beads. In addition three small beads are at the beginning. On these three, the petitioner makes the sign of the cross, recites an act of contrition, and sings the hymn *Come Holy Ghost.*

In each group the Glory Be is said on the seven small beads, an Our Father and Hail Mary on the two large beads. On the last two large beads are prayed the Apostle's Creed and an Our Father and Hail Mary for the intention of the Holy Father.

There is a mystery for each group for reflection:

The first mystery: By the Holy Ghost is Jesus conceived of the Blessed Virgin Mary.

The second: The Spirit of the Lord rested upon Jesus.

The third: By the Spirit is Jesus led into the desert.

The fourth: The Holy Spirit in the church (Pentecost).

The fifth: The Holy Spirit in the soul of the just person.

CHAPLET OF THE SACRED HEART

The chaplet consists of five groups of beads, six small and one large. To begin, make the sign of the cross and pray the Anima Christi:

Soul of Christ, sanctify me.
Body of Christ, save me.
Blood of Christ, inebriate me.
Water from the side of Christ, wash me.

Passion of Christ, strengthen me.
O good Jesus, hear me.
Within your wounds hide me.
Suffer me not to be separated from you.
From the malicious enemy defend me.
In the hour of my death call me.
And bid me come unto you.
That with your saints I may praise you.
For ever and ever. Amen.

On the large bead pray: Sweetest heart of Jesus, I implore that I may love thee more and more.

On the six small beads pray: Sweet heart of Jesus, be my love.

At end of the six beads pray: Sweet heart of Mary, be my salvation.

At the end of praying the fifth group of prayers, conclude with: May the sweet heart of Jesus in the Blessed Sacrament be blessed, loved, and adored, in every tabernacle throughout the world at every moment until the end of time. Amen.

CHAPLET OF THE DIVINE MERCY

The chaplet consists of five groups of ten small beads. Before the small bead of each group is one large bead. Begin with one Our Father, one Hail Mary, and the Apostle's Creed.

On the single bead pray:
Eternal Father, I offer you the body and blood, soul and divinity of your dearly beloved Son, our Lord Jesus Christ, in atonement for our sins and those of the whole world.

On the ten beads pray:
For the sake of his sorrowful passion, have mercy on us and on the whole world.

Closing prayer (Pray three times):
Holy God, holy mighty One, holy immortal One, have mercy on us, and on the whole world.

In wearing a crucifix or a medal the person asks for the prayers of a saint or Mary. When people use these items they should reflect upon their meaning and ask for grace to follow God.

Other articles that are of great assistance to Catholics are sacramentals—blessed water, salt, oil, and candles. The Catholic church believes that these items, having received special blessings, contain the power to protect those who use them from satanic harassment. Sacramentals are not to be regarded in a superstitious way. When used properly in a spirit of prayer, they help purify a person's life.

It is easier to live a Christian life if a person has friends who are also following Christ. They can be a support in times of trouble. It also is wise to have a prayer partner with whom one prays on a regular basis. Joining a prayer group also fosters Christian friendship.

Christians are to take a firm stand against Satan. "Be sober, be watchful. Your adversary the devil prowls around like a roaring lion, seeking some one to devour. Resist him, firm in your faith, knowing that the same experience of suffering is required of your brotherhood throughout the world" (1 Pt 5:8-9).

Christian reading assists spiritual growth. It can be writings of the saints, books on prayer, or any work that draws one closer to God. Such study can educate the reader to discern what is not of God.

"God so loved the world that he gave his only Son, that whoever believes in him should not perish but may have eternal life" (Jn 3:16). If you or anyone you know has been involved in the occult, remember God still loves you and them. All God asks is repentance. He will welcome you back to himself with open arms. Even if you have been involved in satanic human sacrifice, God still loves you. Jesus always forgives and loves.

Who shall separate us from the love of Christ? Shall tribulation, or distress, or persecution, or famine, or nakedness, or peril, or sword? As it is written, "For thy sake we are being killed all the day long; we are regarded as sheep to be slaughtered." No, in all these things we are more than conquerors through him who loved us. *For I am sure that neither death, nor life, nor angels, nor principalities, nor things present, nor things to come, nor powers, nor height, nor depth, nor anything else in all creation, will be able to separate us from the love of God in Christ Jesus our Lord.* Rom 8:35-39, emphasis mine

HELPING TEENS STAY OUT OF SATANISM

Fr. James LeBar, the occult consultant to the archdiocese of New York, states that: "Church leaders—without panicking—need to realize that the satanism fad is serious business. Young people's minds are being influenced and manipulated. Our society and sometimes even we in the church take great pains not to unduly indoctrinate children with godly influences for fear of pressuring them. But no spiritual guidance leaves only emptiness. What we must realize is that the empty space in them is being filled."[4]

Parents are responsible for educating their children not only in the ways of the world, but those of God. Through the proper balance of love and discipline, a child learns to live a moral life. Without proper guidance, a child is more suscetible to occult influences. Part of the guidance that parents are to give is teaching their children the reality of God's love for them.

To know if their teenager is becoming involved in satanism, parents need to educate themselves. One method of discovering what is happening in your area is to go to the local library and see how often occult literature is being checked out, perhaps gently inquiring of a librarian if young people are among those taking it home.

It's also a good idea to check with animal protection services to see if animal mutilations are taking place in the area.

If they are, you may be sure satanic rituals are. Also ask health officials if they have a care unit for occult trauma victims and if it is being used frequently.

If a teenager is involved in a suspect group it is easy to evaluate objectively whether the group is practicing satanism. The following are some marks of a destructive cult—occult or otherwise—adapted from Cult Awareness Network materials:

1. There is undue influence from group leadership, evidence of attempts at mind control.
2. There is charismatic leadership, even a younger person who claims special knowledge and is given special power and privilege in the group.
3. Deception pervades the group's activities. They claim one thing and are obviously something else. They present odd and inconsistent stories about what they do as a group, where they've been.
4. The group exults in exclusivity, elitism, and euphoria. Again, the group is guarded or vague about activities and purposes.
5. Alienation is encouraged by the group. Far beyond the normal teenage drive for independence, participants in these cult-like groups estrange themselves from family, old friends, and society.
6. There may be signs of exploitation in the group. A member may suggest they owe the group something such as money or a favor. Signs of exploitation can include physical abuse, demands for accomplishing certain dangerous tasks as payment or penance, blackmail, and a period of ostracism from the group.[5]

Times in a person's life when she or he is more susceptible to a cult-like group are: after graduating from a school and in the first year of school away from home; anytime a teenager is new to a school or group; and during periods of trauma, like divorce or a family crisis.

To discover if teenagers are dabbling in satanism, ask specific questions about the occult. If you receive specific answers, ask them their source of information. Be mindful of an overemphasized interest in the occult. Look for occult literature. Also look for items that would be used in a satanic sacrifice. These are black robes, black or red candles, books on the occult, jewelry with satanic symbols, and posters with satanic symbols.[6] Also look for a chalice or goblet and odd-shaped knives. Look for a table or compartment in a closet that may be serve as a satanic altar. Look for a *Book of Shadows*. Also called grimoire, it is a journal kept by a person or group. In it are recorded the activities of the person or group and the incantations used in rituals.

A parent's searching of a teenager's room may sound like an invasion of privacy. But if a parent suspects satanic dabbling, then it is the parent's duty to search the room. The goal is to prevent the destruction of the teenager's life. Jerry Johnston shares the following advice: "Respect a teenager's privacy as you would that of any adult, but when you suspect that privacy is misused, remember it's your house. Search your teenager's personal things if you think he or she is signing his or her life away to satanism.... Try this analogy; it might make it easier: You give Joey $50 for this month's lunch money. You find Joey bought crack or PCP angel dust with most of the money. Now, crack or PCP is going to eat Joey's lunch; so it makes sense since Joey violated your trust to take back the rest of the money and refuse to give him more until he proves he can handle your trust again."[7]

Parents must be watchful of their teenager's personality and behavior. Strong behavioral or personality changes could be signs of involvement in a cult or occult group. Be aware of a decided withdrawal from longtime friends and family, signs of self-mutilation or occult symbols tattooed onto the skin, a sudden and consistent switch to dark clothing, notable increase in aggressive behavior, chronic depression, a preoccupation with death and destruction, and nightmares about demons. A parent also needs to be watchful if the teenager has an obsessive interest in heavy metal bands that push satanic themes. A lot of missing pets in the neighborhood may indicate satanic cult activity.

If a teenager is dabbling in satanism, it is important for both the teen and parent to seek reputable counseling. It is also important that any satanic objects be destroyed. Satanic books should be burned. Parents have a right to remove destructive items from their homes.

It is also wise to search the teenager's locker at school. If school authorities object, get a letter from the therapist or law enforcement officer that will allow you to search the locker. The idea is to get all influences of satanism away from the teenager. It is also important to rededicate the home to Jesus Christ through some type of prayer or blessing of the house.

It would be good for both the parent and teenager to speak with a priest or minister—one who understands the dangers of occult involvement. The selection of the clergy-person is important because not all clergy believe in the power of Satan or satanic cults. These steps are essential if the spiritual as well as psychological needs of the teenager and family are to be examined and handled with sensitivity.

And always remember to love, for love heals. Teenagers need parents who will listen to them. They yearn for their loving attention, even if they do not show it. Everyone needs to be affirmed. The majority of teenagers involved in satanism lack love and affirmation in their lives. "A teenager who finds encouragement, love, understanding, responsibility, relationships to emulate, spiritual substance, consistent and loving discipline, training in critical thinking, openness to discuss tough issues such as sex, social training, wisdom, integrity, and attention at home, won't risk all that just to gut chickens and beg for demon possession."[8]

The good news is that through a life of prayer and on-going spiritual warfare we can successfully combat the occult. Further, with some understanding and strategy on satanism and how it operates in the youth culture, we can help our teenagers stay out of the occult.

But what if we suspect that a loved one or friend is diabolically possessed? What can we do? What does the church teach about possession? Does it actually occur? Or is it is simply the grist of sensational horror movies? We discuss possession in our last chapter and also the value of deliverance prayer.

TEN

Diabolical Possession and Deliverance

D IABOLICAL POSSESSION is a very complicated phenomenon. To answer the question, "Am I possessed?", three areas need to be examined: demonology, psychiatry, and parapsychology.[1] Demonology is the study of Satan, the demonic spirits, and their relation to people and the world. To study demonology one must first believe there are demonic spirits. The Catholic church always has taught the existence of personal spirits who are evil through their own choice. There is no reason to examine the possibility of possession if someone denies the reality of demonic spirits.

I believe that to deny the existence of demonic spirits is to deny the integrity of Jesus himself and the Bible. Jesus cannot err. Jesus speaks openly about the devil. Jesus never encouraged belief in superstitions. It would be absurd to think that Jesus went along with people's superstition in talking about demons. Jesus cast out demonic spirits. The Gospels clearly distinguish between Jesus healing a sickness and Jesus expelling a demon. Fifty-one passages in the Bible speak of demons being expelled.[2] Jesus also gave authority to his followers to cast out demons. That power is different from the power to heal the sick.

Psychiatry cannot answer all questions regarding diabolical possession. Some of the phenomena are parapsychological, which falls out of the psychological realm. Parapsychology cannot answer all of the questions. Only an approach that integrates the psychological, parapsychological, and spiritual realms will explain the phenomena of diabolical possession.

DETERMINING DIABOLICAL POSSESSION

Monsignor Corrado Balducci, an expert in diabolical possession, divides diabolical activity into two types, ordinary and extraordinary. Ordinary diabolical activity is temptation. The devil entices people to turn away from God through sin. Extraordinary diabolical activity is divided into three types: *local infestation, personal infestation, and diabolical possession.*[3]

Local infestation is diabolic activity that is in direct and immediate contact with inanimate objects, plants, or animals. The demonic spirits use these to try to influence human beings.[4] Maybe one senses a presence of evil in a certain place or object. The Catholic church consecrates the ground before a church is built upon it. People involved in satanism can and do consecrate ground to Satan.

Personal infestation happens when the devil focuses his power and activity on a person. But remember—*the devil does not have the power to control anyone's intellect and will.*[5] Some people may experience Satan's focus as a particularly strong and persistent temptation. A psychological obsession is different from this temptation. An evil reality is the cause of this sort of temptation, not psychological traumas.

Diabolical possession occurs when the devil has such control over the body of an individual that he or she becomes, as it were, a blind and docile instrument of his perverse and despotic power. The devil can afflict the body, but *he cannot touch the purely spiritual faculties of intellect and will, except indirectly through some bodily sense or faculty.*[6]

The devil is a created being. He has limitations. These limitations will be determined by three factors: the nature of a purely spiritual being, the individual characteristics of each demon, and the will of God.[7]

In chapter two I explained that Satan and demonic spirits are fallen angels. They have a supra-human, not a supernatural, power. Supernatural power is God's alone. Scripture speaks of different types of angels. There also are different types of demons, who could be thought of as possessing different degrees of wickedness. Since God is sovereign, the devil has power only because God permits it. God will not allow people to be tested beyond their strength (1 Cor 10:13). God has total control.

How does a person become open for demonic oppression? Fr. Richard McAlear and Mrs. Betty Brennan, experts in demonic oppression, indicate four ways it can happen:

First, a demonic spirit can attach itself to someone through a wound or trauma. Fr. McAlear calls this a ministering spirit. Secondly, a spirit can attach itself to a person through a repeated sinful action or sinful tendencies. This is a cardinal spirit. One way to remember some cardinal spirits is to remember the capital sins—that is, lust, pride, gluttony, sloth, envy, covetousness, and anger. These sins are against the cardinal virtues of prudence, justice, temperance, and fortitude. These virtues are the hinges of other virtues. Just as other virtues are in some way tied to the four cardinal virtues, so some spirits are tied to, or hinge upon, the cardinal spirits.

A third way is through a person's generational heritage. People inherit their make-up from their parents—their physical attributes, mental abilities, psychological makeup, and spiritual characteristics. If parents have been involved in the occult, generational openness for oppression will be passed along to their children. Exodus 20:5-6 states that a father's wickedness is passed on to his children for four generations, but blessings for a thousand generations upon the faithful.

Finally, a demonic spirit can attach itself to a person through involvement in the occult.[8] Prayer and repentance can bring freedom from the oppression of Satan. People need to close the doors in their lives that are open to demonic oppression. How can these doors be closed? I will explain how a little later in this chapter when I discuss the deliverance prayer.

Diabolic possession is very rare. Why does God allow the devil to possess human beings? One reason is to demonstrate his power. John 9:2-3: "'Rabbi, who sinned, this man or his parents, that he was born blind?' Jesus answered, 'It was not that this man sinned, or his parents, but that the works of God might be made manifest in him.'"

A second reason is to prove the truth of the Christian faith, which is the only religion which asserts believers have been given power over the evil spirits.[9] The Fathers of the Church used this argument to demonstrate the truth of the Catholic faith.

Third, God can permit possession for the ultimate spiritual benefit of the victim. St. John Chrysostom explained that possessed persons can obtain a twofold benefit from their condition. In the first place, they can become more holy and good. Second, having paid the debt for their sins here on earth, they can present themselves pure before the Lord.[10]

A fourth reason for possession is for the conversion of those who come in touch with the possessed person. By seeing the power of the devil, they may come into repentance. Also in experiencing the power of the church through exorcism, they may be converted to belief in God. Lastly, God may also permit diabolical possession as a punishment for sins of the individual, but this would be an exceptional case (1 Cor 5:5).

CHARACTERISTICS OF THE POSSESSED

I will be following Monsignor Corrado Balducci's explanation of the criteria for diabolical possession. It is important to keep an open mind and use the virtue of prudence when looking at these. People should be wary of two extremes: denying everything or being too eager to believe in the activity of the devil.

A characteristic of a possessed person is to have a strong and sometimes violent aversion to the sacred. This aversion to things of God is qualitatively different from that of people who no longer practice a religion. Aversion in the possessed is a vehement hatred expressed spontaneously and violently with facial expressions of rage, a complete transformation of one's features, or convulsive movements of the body. An entirely different personality emerges and alternates with the possessed person's normal one.[11]

That alone does not prove possession but causes one to suspect the presence of diabolical activity. Observing aversion to the sacred is the starting point for the examination of other phenomena in the person.

To determine possible possession, both the psychiatric and parapsychological phenomenology of possession must be considered.[12] In possession, the devil exercises total control over the body of the person. It is not the person who is acting, but the devil working through his or her body. Some actions may be similar to those of mental illness.

> In persons who are mentally ill, the symptoms may be manifested in a variety of ways, depending on the dominant or obsessive ideas that determine them. But in cases of possession there will always be the strong aversion to the sacred or anything that was a source of spiritual consolation and help to the individual; and in many cases the aversion may extend to the moral and physical order.
>
> In authentic cases of diabolical possession the individual may give evidence of his or her abnormal state by facial changes and distortions, by complete relaxation or rigidity of the body. When asked to perform some act of piety or devotion, the patient will react in a more or less violent manner, with contortions of body members, threats and frightening shouts, or with provocative, blasphemous, or sacrilegious mannerisms.[13]

In possession, the devil is acting in the person. His power is greater than human power because of his spiritual nature. The following phenomena experienced in possession are classified as parapsychological: to be able to remain in a very unstable (difficult) posture for a long period of time; to perform actions perfectly with the eyes closed; to do things that one has never learned, such as understanding languages previously unknown; to have occult knowledge of persons, objects, or events that are long past, hidden, or at a great distance. Sometimes the person may levitate, or even fly through the air, performing acrobatic actions. Sometimes the person can move objects without touching them. The person may also cause doors and windows to open and close that are at a great distance from him or her without touching them. The person can also shatter objects at a great distance. These phenomena are beyond all psychic power. Many of these manifestations are similar to the phenomena that are being investigated in parapsychology.[14]

In examining a possible case of possession, one must work from the supposition that all phenomena have a natural explanation. There are similarities between psychiatric and parapsychological phenomena and the symptoms of diabolic possession. A person cannot simply study the phenomena themselves and conclude that a person is possessed. The only valid proof of a case of possible diabolic possession must be based upon an examination of the pattern and style of the phenomena.[15] The book *Satan's Harvest* tells the story of a case of possible diabolic possession.

This book is the story of Maurice Theriault. He experienced many symptoms of diabolic possession. He demonstrated a supra-human strength in lifting tractors on his farm. He experienced periods of his life in which he had no control over what he did, as if there was some other being doing things in his body. He was able to cause objects to fly around the house without touching them. Sometimes at night his wife would find his back covered with blood for no apparent reason. At times, blood would, for no natural reason, seep from his eyes and nostrils. The intensity of these phenomena, along with a strong aversion to anything sacred, made him a strong case for possible diabolic possession.[16]

When a person demonstrates psychiatric problems and parapsychological activity (similar to the case of Maurice Theriault) there is an indication of a possible diabolical possession *if the person also has a strong aversion to the sacred.* If that aversion is not present, there can be no diabolic possession. Psychiatric phenomena and parapsychological phenomena can exist separately. When both phenomena occur in the same person that is exceptional. It is very rare for both sets of phenomena to be accompanied by an intense aversion to the sacred.[17] Remember—in a case of possible diabolic possession all evidence must be gathered and then evaluated.

Only in those few cases in which both psychic and parapsychological phenomena are verified—two or three out of one hundred—should one proceed to the second step of evaluation. The question for this examination: are the psychiatric and parapsychological phenomena explainable by natural means?[18]

Are the person's psychological problems due to his or her life history? Heredity to a great degree influences pathological mental states. Therefore, it is important to investigate the history of the patient and possible mental defects in the family history. The patient's symptoms generally will fall into a given clinical syndrome. But *in cases of diabolical possession, the psychiatric symptoms of the person are different from the psychiatric problem that is expressed.* The symptoms demonstrate a given psychiatric syndrome, but the person demonstrates a different problem.[19]

In the parapsychological realm, the possessed person's parapsychological abilities will be characterized by spontaneity and intensity. Studies of occult phenomena have revealed that some persons have been able to act beyond the limits of normal human powers. This takes a planned concentration. These people experience an exhaustion or tiredness after the parapsychological demonstration. But *the parapsychological demonstration of possessed persons is a spontaneous action. And they do not experience any exhaustion or tiredness after a parapsychological demonstration.*[20]

In union with these areas of phenomena is the aversion to the sacred. This aversion is not casual or thoughtless. It is a constant aversion. In addition, there is an amazing intuitive perception of the sacred and divine. A possessed person may decide, reluctantly, to genuflect before the Blessed Sacrament rather than kiss an image of the Blessed Virgin Mary. It would be extremely difficult for that person to show any sign of respect or reverence to a priest. That would be too great an act of humiliation for the devil.[21]

People who are victims of personal infestation always retain consciousness and control of their own actions. They do not manifest the aversion to the sacred that is characteristic of diabolical possession. A possible case of diabolical possession is to be examined carefully and prudently. After all the data has been collated, a decision can be made. Contained in this decision will be the type of therapy that is required. The proper person to make this judgment is a priest.

Because of the psychiatric and parapsychological phenomena involved in diabolic possession, it is indispensable for the priest exorcist to have some knowledge of psychiatry and parapsychology. After the psychiatrist, parapsychologist, and physician have given their input, the priest exorcist should conclude the diagnostic examination and render the final decision.[22] If it is decided that the patient is diabolically possessed, an exorcism may be performed, but only with permission of the bishop.

MEANS OF DELIVERANCE

Deliverance prayer is one of the oldest traditions of the Catholic church. In the Our Father we pray, "Deliver us from evil." That prayer is a prayer for deliverance. Christians are able to pray for deliverance from evil spirits because Jesus gave them that power. In Luke 10 Jesus commissioned the seventy disciples to spread the kingdom of God. In this action Jesus gave them authority over demonic spirits. The seventy, upon their return to Jesus, exclaimed, "Even the demons are subject to us in your name!"

Though Jesus gave his followers such power, it is up to individual Christians to use it. One of the proofs of the validity of the Catholic church in the early centuries was its power to take authority over or even cast out demonic spirits.

Deliverance prayer is not exorcism. There are two forms of exorcism: solemn and private. Solemn exorcism is a liturgical rite and public action of the Catholic church. Solemn exorcism is performed only by an official delegate of the bishop.

Private exorcism is not a public, liturgical rite. The terms private (or simple) exorcism and deliverance refer to the same action. This style of prayer is used to curb the influence of Satan in the lives of Christians. Whereas in solemn exorcism only the delegate of the bishop may perform the exorcism, any Christian can say the deliverance prayer.

Deliverance prayer is said in the name of the person of Jesus. Solemn exorcism is prayed in the name of Jesus and the whole Catholic church. It would seem logical that a priest, by the power of the Sacrament of Holy Orders, has a greater commission than the laity to pray the deliverance prayer. This is not always the case, however, because this prayer is a charism. God can give charisms to whomever he chooses. Even so, there are certain guidelines to be followed in this type of prayer.

In 1986, in response to some questionable activities, the Sacred Congregation for the Doctrine of Faith published the following statement:

1. Canon 1172 of the Canonical Code declares that nobody can legitimately perform exorcisms on possessed persons, unless he obtains a special and appropriate permission from the territorial Bishop, and determines that this permission be given by the territorial Bishop only to a priest endowed with piety, knowledge, prudence, and integrity of life. The Bishops, therefore, are earnestly asked to demand the observance of these rules.
2. It follows from these rules, that even the faithful may not be allowed to make use of the formula of exorcism against Satan and his fallen angels, taken from the on that was made public by order of the Pope Leo XIII

much less to use the whole text of this exorcism. The Bishops ought to inform the faithful about this matter if the case demands.

3. Finally, for the same reasons, the Bishops are requested to watch that, even in cases where a true diabolical possession is excluded, those who lack the proper permission do not supervise or direct the assemblies in which prayers are used to obtain a releasing, in the course of which the devils are disturbed and their identities are sought.

However, the declaration of these norms by no means should keep the faithful from praying to be delivered from evil, as Jesus taught. Moreover, the Bishops will be able to use any given opportunity to recall what the tradition of the Church teaches about the role played by the sacraments and the intervention of the Blessed Virgin Mary, of the Angels, and of the Saints in the spiritual struggle of Christians against evil spirits.

In examination of these norms, I stress again that only an authorized priest may perform exorcisms. A distinction must be made between exorcism and deliverance prayer. Exorcism is an official action of the church. Deliverance is the private action of an individual in the name of Jesus. The above letter also does not mention silent exorcism, which can be a very powerful prayer. In the Sacrament of Reconciliation, priests are encouraged to use silent exorcism when it will be beneficial to the penitent.

Deliverance should *never* be done in a large group setting. It is best that this prayer be prayed silently. Since the prayer of deliverance rests on the authority of Jesus, there is no need to shout. Shouting does not make Jesus any more powerful. The following is a schema for deliverance prayer:

with praise and thanks to God.

r the protection of everyone present and all family members.

the intercession of Mary and the saints.

power of Satan and demonic spirits.

5. Pray a deliverance prayer quietly. If a person has the charismatic gift of word of knowledge or discernment of spirits, he or she may know the name of a spirit, for example, a spirit of fear. The prayer prayed silently then would be: "In the name of Jesus I command the spirit of fear to leave this person immediately and go directly to the cross where Jesus will do with you as he wills."
6. After the deliverance prayer, pray that the Holy Spirit will come upon the person, bringing healing and filling him or her with grace.

Admittedly, this is only a brief outline of one possible approach to deliverance. For a more in-depth presentation on deliverance, please see *Deliverance from Evil Spirits,* by Fr. Michael Scanlan, T.O.R., and Randall Cirner, which was recommended in the last chapter and is listed in the bibliography. Overall they present a balanced and pastorally sensitive approach to deliverance that is faithful to Catholic teaching.

STORIES OF DELIVERANCE

Following are four stories of praying for deliverance and inner healing. These examples will relate to the four ways a person opens the door for demonic oppression, mentioned earlier:

1. Example of a spirit that attaches itself to a traumatic event in a person's life: Vicki had come to see me for counseling and inner healing prayer. She told me that she had suicidal thoughts repeatedly, but had never tried to act upon them. The thoughts were becoming more troubling. She had discussed them with other counselors, but none seemed to help.

Through prayer I discerned that a spirit of depression was oppressing her. I could have quietly commanded the spirit, but that would have been incomplete. The wound that the spirit was attached to would also need to be healed for her t become whole. It does not do any good to free somer through deliverance prayer if one does not pray for healing of the wound.

When Vicki was six years old she was climbing up on her mother's antique hutch. When she neared the top, the hutch fell over on her. She remembered screaming for help. She thought she was going to die. At that moment, the spirit of depression attached itself to that traumatic wound. I quietly prayed deliverance from the spirit. Then we invited Jesus into her situation. Jesus healed the trauma, and Vicki has not had any more suicidal thoughts. Vicki was freed through deliverance prayer *and* inner healing. Again, it is wrong to pray deliverance without prayer also for inner healing.

2. Example of a cardinal spirit: Remember, a cardinal spirit oppresses a person because the door has been opened through a repeated sinful action. The best prayer for this situation is the Sacrament of Reconciliation (confession). In hearing confession I have often silently prayed deliverance with great effect for the person. But the person's life must also change to remain free from oppression. For example, if a man has been freed from a spirit of lust, he would need to stay away from pornographic material. If he returns to it, the spirit will return.

3. Oppression due to generational bondage: Sometimes when a person is conceived, a seal is made that needs to be broken. A seal is a spiritual characteristic. Think of a letter that has been sealed with wax. Once the seal is broken, the letter can be opened. When parents have been involved in the occult the children receive a seal, an invitation to oppression.

James had come to me because he had trouble praying. He shared that his parents had been involved in witchcraft before he was born. When in our prayer I broke the seal of ⁓ ᶠrom his generational bondage, he felt a burden ᵉd off his shoulders. Prayer has been much easᵢ since that deliverance prayer.

t DeGrandis in his book *Intergenerational Healing* w people's heredity can influence their lives. He has some beautiful, powerful prayers in his book, which I highly recommend. I often use them in dealing with generational issues.

4. Example of oppression received through an occult experience: To break the power of the occult a person needs to repent. Catholics in the occult should go to the Sacrament of Reconciliation. Sometimes all a person needs is a *good confession* to be set free.

To break the power of an occult spirit one needs to have the power of the keys of the kingdom of heaven. This is the power of the priesthood. A lay person should never attempt to break this power alone. If a priest is not available, a small select group would be appropriate. Extreme caution must be used so that no one suffers adverse after-effects of this style of prayer.

Elena, thirty-five years old, needed help. A friend had told her to go to a person who had "special powers" to help her. That person was a santero. (Santeria is explained in chapter six.) Innocently, Elena had paid the santero thousands of dollars, but received no peace from oppression.

Someone referred her to me. Her problem was not just going to the santero. Her parents and two of her brothers also had been involved in the occult, so she had a generational bondage. When she was young, she was spiritually offered to a demonic spirit as a sacrifice to save the life of another child who was sick. When we first met, she was not practicing her Catholic faith.

Elena's case was so involved that I asked a couple of other priests and a man with a powerful gift of prayer and discernment of spirits to assist me. It took a lot of prayer and fasting, but God moved powerfully and set her free. She is now a faithful Catholic attending Mass and receiving Communion. Her new life is a witness to the power of God.

In every case that I have dealt with, the people oppressed by demonic spirits had experienced trauma in their lives. The deeper their involvement in the occult, the more tragic was their wound. People who have been severely hurt need much love and prayer to be free and healed. Remember— God is in charge. God is love. God desires that his people be free from oppression.

I cannot emphasize enough that when people pray for any type of deliverance, they must also pray for inner healing, asking Jesus to fill the person with his love. I suggest that everyone begin praying that God will raise up competent teams, with priests as part of them, for the ministry of deliverance and healing.

It is God himself who brings a person out of darkness into his glorious light through deliverance and healing prayer. The liberated person is given new strength to follow him. Persons who are freed from satanic forces and do not turn over their lives to Jesus, however, will lose their deliverance and healing. Those who pray for deliverance and inner healing are responsible for teaching these people how to follow God.

CONCLUSION

There are two inclinations regarding evil in the modern world. One inclination is to deny the reality of Satan. The other is to attribute everything that is evil to demonic activity. Both are extremes. A Christian needs a balanced approach to the reality of Satan and demonic spirits that neither denies the existence of Satan nor exaggerates his influence and power. No one need be afraid of Satan. Those of us who follow Jesus Christ can claim the authority that Jesus has given us over Satan and demonic spirits. We, with the seventy disciples, can rejoice, "Lord, even the demons are subject to us in your name!" (Lk 10:17).

Scripture References on Satan

In the Bible the proper name Satan first appears in the book of Job.

> Now there was a day when the sons of God came to present themselves before the LORD, and Satan also came among them. The LORD said to Satan, "Whence have you come?" Satan answered the LORD, "From going to and fro on the earth, and from walking up and down on it." And the LORD said to Satan, "Have you considered my servant Job, that there is none like him on the earth, a blameless and upright man, who fears God and turns away from evil?" Then Satan answered the LORD, "Does Job fear God for nought? Hast thou not put a hedge about him and his house and all that he has, on every side? Thou hast blessed the work of his hands, and his possessions have increased in the land. But put forth thy hand now, and touch all that he has, and he will curse thee to thy face." And the LORD said to Satan, "Behold, all that he has is in your power; only upon himself do not put forth your hand." So Satan went forth from the presence of the LORD. Jb 1:6-12

Satan and demonic spirits are at enmity with the followers of the Lord. He (Satan) is the accuser of the human race.

> Then he showed me Joshua the high priest standing before the angel of the LORD, and Satan standing at his right hand to accuse him. And the LORD said to Satan, "The LORD rebuke you, O Satan! The LORD who has chosen Jerusalem rebuke you! Is not this a brand plucked from the fire?" Zec 3:1-2

And

> For God created man for incorruption and made him in the image of his own eternity, but through the devil's envy death

entered the world, and those who belong to his party experience it. **Wis 2:23-24**

The following Gospel passages demonstrate that the ministry of deliverance (the casting out of demonic spirits from people) was a normal part of Jesus' earthly ministry.

"... There was in their synagogue a man with an unclean spirit; and he cried out..." (Mk 1:23-27, parallel passage Lk 4:33-36).

"And he healed many who were sick with various diseases, and cast out many demons..." (Mk 1:34, parallel passages Mt 8:16; Lk 4:41).

"And he went throughout all Galilee, preaching in their synagogues and casting out demons" (Mk 1:39, parallel passage Mt 4:24; Lk 4:18).

"And whenever the unclean spirits beheld him, they fell down before him and cried out, 'You are the Son of God'" (Mk 3:11, parallel passages Lk 6:18; Mt 4:24).

In the parable of the seed Jesus says, "And these are the ones along the path, where the word is sown; when they hear, Satan immediately comes and takes away the word which is sown in them" (Mk 4:15, parallel passages Lk 8:12; Mt 13:19).

"They came to the other side of the sea, to the country of the Gerasenes. And when he had come out of the boat, there met him out of the tombs a man with an unclean spirit..." (Mk 5:1-13, parallel passages Mt 8:28-34; Lk 8:26-36).

"And he called to him the twelve, and began to send them out two by two, and gave them authority over the unclean spirits.... And they cast out many demons, and anointed with oil many that were sick and healed them" (Mk 6:7-13, parallel passages Lk 9:1-6; Mt 10:1,7).

"... And he entered a house, and would not have any one know it; yet he could not be hid. But immediately a woman, whose little daughter was possessed by an unclean spirit, heard of him.... And she went home, and found the child lying in bed, and the demon gone" (Mk 7:24-30, parallel passage Mt 15:21-28).

"And one of the crowd answered him, 'Teacher, I brought my son to you, for he has a dumb spirit' ... And when Jesus saw that a crowd came running together, he rebuked the unclean spirit, saying to it, 'You dumb and deaf spirit, I command you, come out of him, and never enter him again'" (Mk 9:17-25, parallel passages Mt 17:14-21; Lk 9:37-43).

"Then a blind and dumb demoniac was brought to him, and he healed him, so that the dumb man spoke and saw" (Mt 12:22, parallel passage Lk 11:14).

"Now he was teaching in one of the synagogues on the sabbath. And there was a woman who had had a spirit of infirmity for eighteen years;... [Jesus] said to her, 'Woman, you are freed from your infirmity'" (Lk 13:10-12).

When a demonic spirit is cast out of a person, if it cannot attach to another person, it will try to return to its former place of habitation:

> When the unclean spirit has gone out of a man, he passes through waterless places seeking rest, but he finds none. Then he says, 'I will return to my house from which I came.' And when he comes he finds it empty, swept, and put in order. Then he goes and brings with him seven other spirits more evil than himself, and they enter and dwell there;... **Mt 12:43-45**

The passage of the Gerasene demoniac demonstrates that demons will struggle to keep what they believe is theirs:

> And one of the crowd answered him, "Teacher, I brought my son to you, for he has a dumb spirit;... I asked your disciples to cast it out, and they were not able." And he answered them, "O faithless generation, how long am I to be with you? How long am I to bear with you? Bring him to me." And they brought the boy to him; and when the spirit saw him, immediately it convulsed the boy,... And when Jesus saw that a crowd came running together, he rebuked the unclean spirit, saying to it, "You dumb and deaf spirit, I command you, come out of him, and never enter him again." And after crying out and convulsing him terribly, it came out, and the boy was like a corpse; so that most of them said, "He is dead." But Jesus took him by the hand and lifted him up, and he arose. And when he had entered the house, his disciples asked him privately, "Why could we not cast it out?" And he said to them, "This kind cannot be driven out by anything but prayer." **Mk 9:17-29**

Demonic spirits have emotions:

> And when he saw Jesus from afar, he ran and worshiped him; and crying out with a loud voice, he said, "What have you to do

with me, Jesus, Son of the Most High God? I adjure you by God, do not torment me." For he had said to him, "Come out of the man, you unclean spirit!" **Mk 5:6-8**

Demonic spirits can speak and demonstrate that they have knowledge.

Then some of the itinerant Jewish exorcists undertook to pronounce the name of the Lord Jesus over those who had evil spirits, saying, "I adjure you by the Jesus whom Paul preaches." Seven sons of a Jewish high priest named Sceva were doing this. But the evil spirit answered them, "Jesus I know, and Paul I know; but who are you?" **Acts 19:13-15**

St. Paul shows that the true follower of Jesus has authority over demons:

As we were going to the place of prayer, we were met by a slave girl who had a spirit of divination and brought her owners much gain by soothsaying. She followed Paul and us, crying, "These men are servants of the Most High God, who proclaim to you the way of salvation." And this she did for many days. But Paul was annoyed, and turned and said to the spirit, "I charge you in the name of Jesus Christ to come out of her." And it came out that very hour. **Acts 16:16-18**

Satan is:

... the son of perdition, who opposes and exalts himself against every so-called god or object of worship, so that he takes his seat in the temple of God, proclaiming himself to be God. Do you not remember that when I was still with you I told you this? And you know what is restraining him now so that he may be revealed in his time. For the mystery of lawlessness is already at work; only he who now restrains it will do so until he is out of the way. And then the lawless one will be revealed, and the Lord Jesus will slay him with the breath of his mouth and destroy him by his appearing and his coming. The coming of the lawless one by the activity of Satan will be with all power and with pretended signs and wonders, and with all wicked deception for those who are to perish, because they refused to love the truth and so be saved. **2 Thes 2:3-10**

Demonic spirits can attack a person's physical body:

Now he was teaching in one of the synagogues on the sabbath. And there was a woman who had had a spirit of infirmity for eighteen years; she was bent over and could not fully straighten herself. And when Jesus saw her, he called her and said to her, "Woman, you are freed from your infirmity." And he laid his hands upon her, and immediately she was made straight, and she praised God. **Lk 13:10-13**

Demonic spirits can affect one's senses or normal physical abilities:

Then a blind and dumb demoniac was brought to him, and he healed him, so that the dumb man spoke and saw. And all the people were amazed.... **Mt 12:22-23**

And

But immediately a woman, whose little daughter was possessed by an unclean spirit, heard of him, and came and fell down at his feet. Now the woman was a Greek, a Syrophoenician by birth. And she begged him to cast the demon out of her daughter.... And she went home, and found the child lying in bed, and the demon gone. **Mk 7:25-30**

The seventy disciples had power over demonic spirits:

The seventy returned with joy saying, "Lord, even the demons are subject to us in your name!" And he said to them, "I saw Satan fall like lightning from heaven. Behold, I have given you authority to tread upon serpents and scorpions, and over all the power of the enemy; and nothing shall hurt you. Nevertheless, do not rejoice in this, that the spirits are subject to you; but rejoice that your names are written in heaven." **Lk 10:17-20**

A demonic spirit may even be allowed to attack a person in order to bring them back to the faith:

... By rejecting conscience, certain persons have made shipwreck of their faith, among them Hymenaeus and Alexander, whom I have delivered to Satan that they may learn not to blaspheme. **1 Tm 1:19-20**

Church Pronouncements and Writings of Early Church Fathers on Satan

CHURCH PRONOUNCEMENTS

The Fourth Lateran Council (A.D. 1215) states:

For the devil and the other demons were indeed created by God naturally good, but they became evil by their own doing. As for man, he sinned at the suggestion of the devil.[1]

The Council of Trent (1546) in its *Decree on Original Sin* states that the devil played a major role in the fall of the first man, Adam.

If anyone does not profess that Adam, the first man, by transgressing God's commandment in paradise, at once lost the holiness and justice in which he had been constituted; and that offending God by his sin, he drew upon himself the wrath and indignation of God and consequently death with which God had threatened him, and together with death captivity in the power of him who henceforth "has the power of death" (Heb 2:14), i.e., the devil; and that "the whole Adam, body and soul, was changed for the worse through the offense of sin," anathema sit.[2]

The Second Vatican Council repeats this teaching in several documents. The *Dogmatic Constitution on the Church* teaches that Satan is the one who deceives human beings and leads them away from God.

But rather often men, deceived by the Evil One, have become caught up in futile reasoning and have exchanged the truth of God for a lie, serving the creature rather than the Creator. (cf. Rom 1:21, 25)[3]

The *Constitution on the Sacred Liturgy* teaches that Jesus was sent to free people from the power of Satan:

Just as Christ was sent by the Father, so also he sent the apostles, filled with the Holy Spirit. This he did so that, by preaching the gospel to every creature (cf. Mk 16:15), they might proclaim that the Son of God, by his death and resurrection, had freed us from the power of Satan (cf. Acts 26:18) and from death, and brought us into the kingdom of His Father. (No. 6)

In the *Decree on the Church's Missionary Activity* the Vatican Council teaches:

In order to establish peace or communion between sinful human beings and Himself as well as to fashion them into a fraternal community, God determined to intervene in human history in a way both new and definitive. For He sent His Son, clothed in our flesh, in order that through this Son He might snatch men from the power of darkness and of Satan (cf. Col 1:13; Acts 10:38) and that in His Son He might reconcile the world to Himself. (No. 3)

And:

But whatever truth and grace are to be found among the nations, as a sort of secret presence of God, this (missionary) activity frees from all taint of evil and restores to Christ its maker, who overthrows the devil's domain and wards off the manifold malice of vice. (No. 9)

The *Pastoral Constitution on the Church in the Modern World* states that the Vatican Council:

... gazes upon that world which is the theater of man's history, and carries the marks of his energies, his tragedies, and his triumphs; that world which the Christian sees as created and sustained by its Maker's love, fallen indeed into the bondage of sin, yet emancipated now by Christ. He was crucified and rose again to break the stranglehold of personified Evil, so that this world might be fashioned anew according to God's design and reach its fulfillment. (No. 2)

Later in this document the Vatican Council describes the inherent dignity of human beings, stating that it was through the prodding of Satan (real personified evil) that humanity sinned:

Although he was made by God in a state of holiness, from the very dawn of history man abused his liberty, at the urging of personified Evil. (No. 13)

Pope Paul VI in a general audience on November 15, 1972 stated:

What are the church's greatest needs at the present time? Don't be surprised at our answer and don't write it off as simplistic or even superstitious: one of the church's greatest needs is to be defended against the evil which we call the Devil.... Evil is not merely an

absence of something but an active force, a living,
that is perverted and that perverts others.... It is a
the picture provided by biblical and church teachi
acknowledge the Devil's existence... or to explain
pseudoreality, a conceptual, fanciful, personification of the unknown causes of our misfortunes.... St. Paul calls him the "god of
this world," and warns us of the struggle we Christians must carry on
in the dark, not only against one Devil, but against a frightening
multiplicity of them.... So we know that this dark, disturbing being
exists, and that he is still at work with his treacherous cunning; he is
the hidden enemy who sows errors and misfortunes in human history.... He undermines man's moral equilibrium with his sophistry.
He is the malign, clever seducer who knows how to make his way
into us through the senses, the imagination and the libido, through
utopian logic, or through disordered social contacts in the give and
take of our activities, so that he can bring in us deviations that are
all the more harmful because they seem to conform to our physical
or mental make-up, or to our profound, instinctive aspirations....

This matter of the Devil and of the influence he can exert on
individuals as well on communities, entire societies or events, is a
very important chapter of Catholic doctrine which should be studied again, although it is given little attention today. Some think a
sufficient compensation can be found in psychoanalytic and psychiatric studies or in spiritualistic experiences, which are unfortunately so widespread in some countries today.[4]

In 1975, the Sacred Congregation for the Doctrine of the Faith
published *Les formes de la superstition* to help the faithful understand
the Catholic church's teaching regarding demonic spirits.

It would be a fatal mistake to act as if history were already finished
and redemption had achieved all its effects, so that it were no
longer necessary to engage in the struggle [against the devil and
demons] of which the New Testament and the masters of the spiritual life speak.... To maintain today, therefore, that Jesus' words
about Satan express only a teaching borrowed from his culture and
are unimportant for the faith of other believers is evidently to show
little understanding either of the Master's character or of his age.
If Jesus used this kind of language and, above all, if he translated it
into practice during his ministry, it was because it expressed a doctrine that was to some extent essential to the idea and reality of the
salvation that he was bringing.... Satan whom Jesus attacked with
his exorcisms and confronted in the wilderness and in his passion,

cannot simply be a product of the human ability to tell stories and personify ideas nor a stray survival of a primitive culture and its language.... Satan's action on man is admittedly interior but it is impossible to regard him as therefore simply a personification of sin and temptation.... It was for all these reasons that the Fathers of the Church were convinced from Scripture that Satan and the demons are the enemies of man's redemption, and they did not fail to remind the faithful of their existence and action.... The assertion that demons exist and have power is not based solely on these mere categorical documents. They find another, more general and less formal expression in conciliar statements every time the condition of man without Christ is described.... It is with this traditional teaching in mind that the Second Vatican Council, being more concerned with the present life of the Church than with the doctrine of creation, did not fail to warn us against the activity of Satan and the demons. Vatican II, like the Councils of Florence and Trent before it, has once again proclaimed with the apostle that Christ came to rescue us "from the power of darkness." ... Elsewhere Vatican II renews the warning issued by the letter to the Ephesians that we must "put on the armor of God so that you may be able to stand firm against the tactics of the devil." For as this same document reminds the laity, "Our battle is not against human forces but against the Principalities and Powers, the rulers of this world of darkness, the evil spirits in the regions above." We are not surprised, finally, to see that, when the council wishes to present the Church as God's kingdom that has already begun, it appeals to the miracles of Jesus and specifically to his exorcisms. For it is precisely with reference to exorcisms that Jesus made the well known statement: "The reign of God is upon you."... The liturgy directly echoes New Testament teaching when it reminds us that the life of the baptized is a struggle, carried on with the grace of Christ and the strength of his Spirit, against the world, the flesh, and the demonic beings.... To sum up: The position of the Catholic Church on demons is clear and firm. The existence of Satan and the demons has, indeed, never been the object of an explicit affirmation by the magisterium but this is because the question was never put in those terms. Heretics and faithful alike, on the basis of Scripture, were in agreement on the existence and chief misdeeds of Satan and his demons. For this reason, when doubt is thrown these days on the reality of the devil we must, as we observed earlier, look to the constant and universal faith of the Church and to its chief source, the teaching of Christ. It is in the teaching of the gospel and in the heart of the faith as lived that the existence of the world of demons is revealed as dogma. The contemporary disaffection which we criticized at the beginning of this essay is, therefore, not simply a challenge to a secondary element of Christian thought but a direct denial of the constant faith of the Church, its way of conceiving redemption and (at the source of both of these) the very consciousness of Jesus himself.[5]

EARLY FATHERS OF THE CHURCH

St. Justin Martyr writes:
For He also become man, as we stated, and was born in accordance with the will of God the Father for the benefit of believers, and for the defeat of demons. Even now, your own eyes will teach you the truth of this last statement. For many demoniacs throughout the world, and even in your own city, were exorcised by many of our Christians in the name of Jesus Christ, who was crucified under Pontius Pilate; and our men cured them, and they still cure others by rendering helpless and dispelling the demons who had taken possession of these men, even when they could not be cured by all the other exorcists, and the exploiters of incantations and drugs.[6]

St. Irenaeus writes:
... those who are in truth his disciples, receiving grace from him, do in his name perform [miracles], so as to promote the welfare of other men, according to the gift which each one has received from him. For some do certainly drive out devils, so that those who have been cleansed from evil spirits frequently both believe [in Christ], and join themselves to the Church.[7]

St. Ignatius of Antioch wrote to the Ephesians:
Be zealous, therefore, to assemble more frequently to render thanks and to praise God. For, when you meet together frequently, the powers of Satan are destroyed and danger from him is dissolved in the harmony of your faith. There is nothing better than peace in which an end is put to the warfare of things in heaven and on earth.[8]

Origen emphasizes the power of a simple prayer using the name of Jesus:
For it is not in incantations that Christians seem to prevail (over evil spirits), but by the name of Jesus, accompanied by the announcement of the narratives which relate to him; for the repetition of these has frequently been the means of driving demons out

of men, especially when those who repeated them did so in a sound and genuinely believing spirit.

Such power, indeed, does the name of Jesus possess over evil spirits, that there have been instances where it was effectual, when it was pronounced even by bad men, which Jesus himself taught [would be the case], when he said: "Any shall say to me in that day, in thy name we have cast out devils and done many wonderful works."[9]

Edwin Hamilton Gifford states in his introduction to the works of Cyril of Jerusalem:

One of the earliest ceremonies, after the registration of names, was exorcism, which seems to have been often repeated during the candidate's course of preparation. "Receive with earnestness the exorcisms: whether thou be breathed upon or exorcised, the act is to thee salvation."[10]

Notes

ONE
Satan in the Bible and Catholic Tradition

1. An exorcism is performed when it is believed that a person is possessed by Satan. Strict rules are to be followed. For a person to receive an exorcism, he or she must first go through a series of psychological examinations. An exorcism is performed only by a competent priest exorcist with the bishop's permission after all examinations have been completed.
2. Rahner, Karl, ed. *Encyclopedia of Theology: The Concise Sacramentum Mundi.* (New York: Crossroad Publishing Company, 1975), 341.
3. Rahner, *Encyclopedia of Theology*, 342.
4. McKenzie, John, S. J., ed., *Dictionary of the Bible* (Englewood Cliffs: Prentice Hall, 1990), 71-72.
5. Harris, Charles, C.S.C., *Resist the Devil* (South Bend: Greenlawn Press, 1988), 4.
6. Martyr, Justin, "Second Apology," tr. by Thomas B. Falls in *The Fathers of the Church, Vol. VI* (New York: Christian Heritage Inc., 1948), 125-126.
7. Irenaeus. "Against Heretics," II, 32, 4, tr. by Alexander Roberts, et al., in *Ante-Nicene Christian Library*, Vol. V (Edinburgh, London: T & T Clark, 1884), 245-246.
8. Ignatius of Antioch. "Letter to the Ephesians," No. 13, *The Fathers of the Church*, 92.
9. Gifford, E. H., "St. Cyril of Jerusalem and St. Gregory Nanzienzen" in *Library of Nicene and Post-Nicene Fathers*, Second Series, Vol. VII (New York: The Christian Literature Company, 1984), XIX.
10. Origen, "Against Celus" in *Ante-Nicene Christian Library*, Vol. X (New York: The Christian Literature Company, 1984), 402.
11. "The Christian Faith in the Doctrinal Documents of the Catholic Church," as cited by Harris, Charles, C.S.C., in *Resist the Devil*, 101.
12. Abbott, Walter, S.J., ed., "The Dogmatic Constitution on the Church" in *The Documents of Vatican II* (New York: Corpus Books, 1966), no. 16.
13. Abbott, "The Dogmatic Constitution on the Sacred Liturgy" in *The Documents of Vatican II*, no. 6.

14. Abbott, "The Decree on the Church's Mission Activity" in *The Documents of Vatican II*, no. 3.

15. Abbott, "The Decree on the Church's Mission Activity" in *The Documents of Vatican II*, no. 9.

16. Abbott, "The Pastoral Constitution on the Church in the Modern World" in *The Documents of Vatican II*, no 2.

17. *L'Osservatore Romano*, English language edition (Rome: November 23, 1972), 3.

18. *The Roman Ritual: Rite of Baptism for Children* (New York: Catholic Book Publishing Company, 1970, 1977), 33.

19. *The Rites of the Catholic Church* (New York: Pueblo Publishing Company, 1976), 75.

20. Flannery, Austin, O.P., *Vatican Council II: More Postconciliar Documents*, as cited in Harris, Charles, C.S.C., in *Resist the Devil*, 105-106.

THREE
Divination

1. *The Encyclopedia of Occultism and Parapsychology*, as cited in Hunt, Stoker, *Ouija, the Most Dangerous Game* (New York: Harper and Row Publishers, 1985), 3.

2. Hunt, *Ouija, the Most Dangerous Game*, 4.

3. Hunt, *Ouija, the Most Dangerous Game*, 4.

4. Hunt, *Ouija, the Most Dangerous Game*, 5-6.

5. McAll, Dr. Kenneth, *Healing the Family Tree* (London: Sheldon Press, 1984), 41–42.

6. Gray, Eden, *The Tarot Revealed* (New York: New American Library, 1988), 11.

7. Gray, *The Tarot Revealed*, 11.

8. Spence, Lewis, *An Encyclopedia of Occultism* (Secaucus: The Citadel Press, 1960), 403.

9. Spence, *An Encyclopedia of Occultism*, 215.

10. Spence, *An Encyclopedia of Occultism*, 215.

11. *The New Encyclopedia Britannica*, Vol. 25 (Chicago: University of Chicago, 1986), 81.

12. Koch, Kurt, *Christian Counseling and Occultism* (Grand Rapids: Kregel Publications, 1972), 85.

13. Koch, *Christian Counseling*, 99.

14. Koch, *Christian Counseling*, 99.

15. *The New Encyclopedia Britannica*, Vol. 25, 80.

16. *The New Catholic Encyclopedia*, Vol. 1 (New York: McGraw Hill Publishers, 1967), 986.

17. *The New Catholic Encyclopedia*, Vol.1, 987.

18. *The New Catholic Encyclopedia*, Vol.1, 988.

19. *The New Encyclopedia Britannica*, Vol. 25, 83.

20. *The New Encyclopedia Britannica*, Vol. 25, 84.

21. Roman, Sanaya, and Parker, Duane, *Opening to Channel* (Tiburon, California: H.J. Kramer, Inc., 1987), 1.
22. Roman, *Opening to Channel*, 42.
23. Roman, *Opening to Channel*, 58.
24. Martin, Walter, *The New Cults* (Ventura, California: Regal Books, 1980), 239.
25. Silva, José, *The Silva Mind Control Method* (New York: Pocket Books, 1977), 93.
26. Silva, *The Silva Mind Control Method*, 94.

FOUR
Transcendental Meditation

1. Maloney, George, S.J., *TM and Christian Meditation* (Pecos, New Mexico: Dove Publications, 1976), 3.
2. Maloney, *TM and Christian Meditation*, 4.
3. Maloney, *TM and Christian Meditation*, 4, 9.
4. Maloney, *TM and Christian Meditation*, 11.
5. Kelsey, Morton, *Discernment: A Study in Ecstasy and Evil* (New York: Paulist Press, 1978), 38.
6. Dr. Elmer Green, Menninger Foundation, Topeka, Kansas, as cited in Maloney, George, S.J., *Prayer of the Heart* (South Bend: Ave Maria Press, 1981), 155.
7. Maloney, *Prayer of the Heart*, 23.
8. Maloney, *Prayer of the Heart*, 30.
9. Maloney, *Prayer of the Heart*, 129.
10. St. Gregory of Sinai, *Instructions to Hesychasts in Writings from the Philokalia on Prayer of the Heart*, as cited in Maloney, *Prayer of the Heart*, 132-133.
11. Maloney, *Prayer of the Heart*, 156.

FIVE
Witchcraft

1. *The New Encyclopedia Britannica*, Vol. 25, 88.
2. *The New Encyclopedia Britannica*, Vol. 25, 93.
3. Dungeons and Dragons (D&D)® is a registered trademark of a fantasy role-playing game which was developed by Gary Gygax. It is manufactured by TSR, Inc.
4. Leithart, Peter and Grant, George, *A Christian Response to Dungeons and Dragons* (Fort Worth, Texas: Dominion Press, 1987), 5.
5. Leithart, *A Christian Response*, 5.
6. Leithart, *A Christian Response*, 5.
7. Leithart, *A Christian Response*, 8.
8. Leithart, *A Christian Response*, 11.
9. *Los Angeles Times* (Los Angeles: January 7, 1984).

SIX

Sorcery

1. *New Catholic Encyclopedia*, Vol. 9, 67.
2. Buckland, Raymond, *Buckland's Complete Book of Witchcraft* (St. Paul: Llewellyn Publications, 1990), 181.
3. Buckland, *Buckland's Complete Book of Witchcraft*, 182.
4. McAlear, Richard, *Conference: Deliverance 1988* (Jacksonville: Christian Healing Ministries, 1988).
5. Brennan, Joseph, *The Kingdom of Darkness* (Lafayette: Acadian House Publishing, 1989), 39-50.
6. Gonzalez-Wippler, Mingene, *Santeria: the Religion* (New York: Harmony Books, 1989), 1.
7. Murphy, Joseph, *Santeria: an African Religion in America* (Boston: Beacon Press, 1988), 21.
8. Murphy, *Santeria: an African Religion in America*, 22.
9. Murphy, *Santeria: an African Religion in America*, 27.
10. Gonzales-Wippler, *Santeria: the Religion*, 3.
11. Murphy, *Santeria: an African Religion in America*, 30.
12. Murphy, *Santeria: an African Religion in America*, 32.
13. Murphy, *Santeria: an African Religion in America*, 35.
14. Murphy, *Santeria: an African Religion in America*, 8.
15. Gonzales-Wippler, *Santeria: the Religion*, 12.
16. Gonzales-Wippler, *Santeria: the Religion*, 12.
17. Gonzales-Wippler, *Santeria: the Religion*, 42.
18. Gonzales-Wippler, *Santeria: the Religion*, 136.
19. Gonzales-Wippler, *Santeria: the Religion*, 41.
20. Gonzales-Wippler, *Santeria: the Religion*, 76.
21. Gonzales-Wippler, *Santeria: the Religion*, 7.
22. Gonzales-Wippler, *Santeria: the Religion*, 108.
23. Gonzales-Wippler, *Santeria: the Religion*, 99-100.
24. Gonzales-Wippler, *Santeria: the Religion*, 165.
25. Gonzales-Wippler, *Santeria: the Religion*, 86.
26. Keating, Karl, *Catholicism and Fundamentalism* (San Francisco: Ignatius Press, 1988), 261.
27. Keating, *Catholicism and Fundamentalism*, 263.

SEVEN

New Age and Neo-Pagan Movements

1. Miller, Elliot, *A Crash Course on the New Age Movement* (Grand Rapids: Baker Book House, 1989), 14-15.
2. Miller, *A Crash Course*, 17.
3. Miller, *A Crash Course*, 17.
4. Groothuis, Douglas, *Unmasking the New Age* (Downers Grove: Intervarsity Press, 1986), 17.
5. Miller, *A Crash Course*, 17.

6. Martin, Walter, *The New Age Cult* (Minneapolis: Bethany House Publishers, 1989), 36.

7. Miller, *A Crash Course*, 28.

8. Creme, Benjamin, *The Reappearance of the Christ and the Masters of Wisdom* (London: The Tara Press, 1980), 135.

9. Spangler, David. *Reflections on the Christ*, 13, as cited in Martin, *The New Age Cults*, 27.

10. Martin, *The New Age Cults*, 27.

11. Creme, *The Reappearance of the Christ and the Masters of Wisdom*, 30.

12. Miller, *A Crash Course*, 30.

13. Martin, Walter, *The New Cults* (Ventura: Regal Books, 1980), 351.

14. Martin, *The New Age Cults*, 95.

15. Chandler, Russell, *Understanding the New Age* (Dallas: Word Publishing, 1988), 252.

16. Groothuis, *Unmasking the New Age*, 135.

17. Groothuis, *Unmasking the New Age*, 135.

18. Montague, George, S.M. *Our Father, Our Mother: Mary and the Faces of God* (Steubenville: Franciscan University Press, 1990), 48-49.

19. Miller, *A Crash Course*, 122.

20. Miller, *A Crash Course*, 165.

21. Miller, *A Crash Course*, 165-166.

22. Baer, Randall, *Inside the New Age Nightmare* (Lafayette: Huntington House Inc., 1989), 104.

23. Baer, *Inside the New Age Nightmare*, 106.

24. Chandler, *Understanding the New Age*, 107-108.

25. Martin, *The New Age Cult*, 91.

26. Martin, *The New Age Cult*, 91-92.

27. Martin, *The New Age Cult*, 92-93.

28. Groothuis, *Unmasking the New Age*, 136.

29. Buckland, *Buckland's Complete Book of Witchcraft*, 9-10.

30. Buckland, *Buckland's Complete Book of Witchcraft*, 18.

31. Montague, *Our Father, Our Mother*, 58.

32. Gonzales-Wippler, Mingene, *A Kabbalah for the Modern World* (St. Paul: Llewellyn Publications, 1987), 2, 5.

33. Gonzales-Wippler, *A Kabbalah for the Modern World*, 38.

34. Gonzales-Wippler, *A Kabbalah for the Modern World*, 4.

35. Gonzales-Wippler, *A Kabbalah for the Modern World*, 54.

36. Gonzales-Wippler, *A Kabbalah for the Modern World*, 115.

37. Beesing, Maria, O.P., et al., *The Enneagram* (Denville: Dimension Books Inc., 1984), 1.

38. Pacwa, Mitch, S.J.,"The Enneagram: Questions that Need Answering" in *New Covenant* (Ann Arbor: February, 1991), 14.

39. Pacwa, "The Enneagram" in *New Covenant*, 14.

40. Martin, *Kingdom of the Cults*, 366.

41. Pacwa, "The Enneagram" in *New Covenant*, 14.

42. Pacwa, "The Enneagram" in *New Covenant*, 14.

43. Pacwa, "The Enneagram" in *New Covenant*, 14.

44. Pacwa, "The Enneagram" in *New Covenant*, 14.

45. Metz, Barbara, S.N.D., et al., *The Enneagram and Prayer* (Denville: Dimension Books Inc., 1987), 20.

46. Rahner, *Encyclopedia of Theology*, 1150.

47. Pacwa, "The Enneagram" in *New Covenant*, 17.

48. Groeschel, Benedict, *Spiritual Passages: The Psychology of Spiritual Development* (New York: Crossroad Publishing Company, 1983), 94-95.

49. Groeschel, *Spiritual Passages*, 96-97.

EIGHT
Satanism

1. Larson, Bob, *Satanism: The Seduction of America's Youth* (Nashville: Thomas Nelson Publishers, 1989), 103-104.

2. Cooper, John Charles, *The Black Mask* (Old Tappan: Fleming H. Revell Company, 1990), 11.

3. Cooper, *The Black Mask*, 11.

4. Cooper, *The Black Mask*, 14.

5. Cooper, *The Black Mask*, 33.

6. Cooper, *The Black Mask*, 3.

7. Cooper, *The Black Mask*, 40.

8. Cooper, *The Black Mask*, 43.

9. Cooper, *The Black Mask*, 47.

10. Crowley, Aleister, *Magick in Theory and Practice* (New York: Dover Publications Inc., 1929), xi.

11. Larson, *Satanism*, 152.

12. Crowley, *Magick*, xxi.

13. Crowley, *Magick*, xxii.

14. Crowley, *Magick*, 56.

15. Crowley, *Magick*, 72-73.

16. Crowley, *Magick*, 168-169.

17. Crowley, *Magick*, 90.

18. Crowley, *Magick*, 95-96.

19. Crowley, *Magick*, 99.

20. Spence, Lawrence, *The History and Origins of Druidism* (Eugene: Publishing Ltd., 1976), 104, as cited in Michaelsen, Johanna, *Like Lambs to the Slaughter*, (Eugene: Harvest House Publishers, 1989), 186.

21. LaVey, Anton, *The Satanic Bible* (New York: Avon Books, 1969), 25.

22. LaVey, *The Satanic Bible*, 88-90.

23. Johnston, Jerry, *The Edge of Evil: The Rise of Satanism in North America* (Dallas: Word Publishing Company, 1989), 151.

24. Johnston, *The Edge of Evil*, 166.

25. Friesen, James Ph.D., *Uncovering the Mystery of MPD* (San Bernardino:

25. Friesen, James Ph.D., *Uncovering the Mystery of MPD* (San Bernardino: Here's Life Publishers, 1991), 79-81.
26. Friesen, *Uncovering the Mystery of MPD*, 81-82.
27. Brennan, *The Kingdom of Darkness*, 29.
28. Johnston, *The Edge of Evil*, 167-168.
29. McAlear, *Conference: Deliverance 1988*.
30. Larson, *Satanism*, 22-23.
31. Johnston, *The Edge of Evil*, 8.
32. Roelofsma, Derk, "Battling Satanism a Haunting Task" in *Insight* (November 1, 1988), 49, as cited in Larson, *Satanism*, 122.
33. *Bakersfield Californian* (January 23, 1987) as cited in Johnston, *The Edge of Evil*, 68.
34. Friesen, *Uncovering the Mystery of MPD*, 96.
35. Johnston, *The Edge of Evil*, 55-56.
36. Johnston, *The Edge of Evil*, 98.
37. Larson, *Satanism*, 87.
38. Brennan, *The Kingdom of Darkness*, 37-38.
39. Brennan, *The Kingdom of Darkness*, 27.
40. Brennan, *The Kingdom of Darkness*, 62.
41. Brennan, *The Kingdom of Darkness*, 63.
42. Brennan, *The Kingdom of Darkness*, 65.
43. Brennan, *The Kingdom of Darkness*, 44.
44. *The Diagnostic and Statistical Manual of Mental Disorders (DSM-III-R)*. (Washington D.C: American Psychiatric Association, 1987), 272.
45. Friesen, *Uncovering the Mystery of MPD*, 62-63.
46. Friesen, *Uncovering the Mystery of MPD*, 42.
47. Friesen, *Uncovering the Mystery of MPD*, 117.
48. Friesen, *Uncovering the Mystery of MPD*, 64.
49. Friesen, *Uncovering the Mystery of MPD*, 66.
50. Friesen, *Uncovering the Mystery of MPD*, 209.
51. Johnston, *The Edge of Evil*, 221-225.
52. Gould, Catherine, Ph.D., Conference on Satanic Ritual Child Abuse (Malibu, California: Pepperdine University, 1986).
53. Gould, Conference in Satanic Ritual Child Abuse.
54. Gould, Conference on Satanic Ritual Child Abuse.
55. Brennan, *The Kingdom of Darkness*, 79.
56. Brennan, *The Kingdom of Darkness*, 48.

NINE
Renouncing the Occult

1. Cruz, Joan Carroll, *Eucharistic Miracles* (Rockford: Tan Books and Publishers Inc., 1987), 3-7.
2. Ensley, Eddie, *Sounds of Wonder* (New York: Paulist Press, 1977), 3.
3. Ensley, *Sounds of Wonder*, 3,14.

4. Johnston, *The Edge of Evil*, 233.
5. Johnston, *The Edge of Evil*, 244-245.
6. Brennan, *The Kingdom of Darkness*, 47.
7. Johnston, *The Edge of Evil*, 246-247.
8. Johnston, *The Edge of Evil*, 249.

TEN
Diabolical Possession and Deliverance

1. Balducci, Corrado, *The Devil*, tr. by Jordan Aumann, O.P. (New York: Alba House, 1990), 74.
2. Balducci, *The Devil*, 79.
3. Balducci, *The Devil*, 93.
4. Balducci, *The Devil*, 93.
5. Balducci, *The Devil*, 93.
6. Balducci, *The Devil*, 94-95.
7. Balducci, *The Devil*, 95.
8. McAlear, *Conference: Deliverance 1988*
9. Balducci, *The Devil*, 118.
10. Balducci, *The Devil*, 119.
11. Balducci, *The Devil*, 127.
12. Balducci, *The Devil*, 128.
13. Balducci, *The Devil*, 129.
14. Balducci, *The Devil*, 130-131.
15. Balducci, *The Devil*, 134.
16. Lasalandra, Michael and Merenda, Mark, *Satan's Harvest* (New York: Dell Publishing, 1990).
17. Balducci, *The Devil*, 135.
18. Balducci, *The Devil*, 136.
19. Balducci, *The Devil*, 138.
20. Balducci, *The Devil*, 139.
21. Balducci, *The Devil*, 140-141.
22. Balducci, *The Devil*, 150.

APPENDIX TWO
Church Pronouncements and Writings of Early Church Fathers on Satan

1. Neuner, J., S.J., and Dupris, J., S.J., *The Christian Faith in the Doctrinal Documents of the Catholic Church*, revised edition (New York: Alba House, 1982), 199, as cited in Harris, *Resist the Devil* (South Bend: Greenlawn Press, 1988), 101.
2. Neuner and Dupris, *The Christian Faith*, 137-138, as cited in Harris, *Resist the Devil*, 102.
3. Abbott, Walter M., ed., *"The Dogmatic Constitution on the Church"* in *The Documents of Vatican II* (New York: Corpus Books, 1966), No. 16. All

further references to the documents of Vatican II in this appendix are from this source. The citations by number refer to section or paragraph numbers in the respective documents.

4. *The Pope Speaks,* Vol. XVII, No. 4 (Washington D.C.: TPS Publications, Winter, 1973), 315-318.

5. Flannery, Austin, O.P. ed., "Les formes de la superstition" in *Vatican Council II: More Post Conciliar Documents* (Northport: Costello Publishing Company, 1982), 456-485.

6. Martyr, Justin, "Second Apology" in *The Fathers of the Church,* Vol. VI, tr. by Thomas B. Falls (New York: Christian Heritage, Inc., 1948), 125-126.

7. Irenaeus, "Against Heretics" in *Ante-Nicene Christain Library,* Vol.V., tr. by Alexander Roberts, et al. (Edinburgh/London: T & T Clark, 1884), 245-246.

8. Ignatius of Antioch, "Letter to the Ephesians" in *The Fathers of the Church,* Falls, No. 13.

9. Origen, "Against Celus" in *Ante-Nicene Christian Library,* Vol. X, Roberts, 402.

10. Gifford, E.H., "St. Cyril of Jerusalem and St. Gregory Nanzienzen" in *Library of Nicene and Post-Nicene Fathers,* Second Series, Vol. VII (New York: The Christian Literature Company, 1984), XIX.

Glossary

666 The mark of the beast mentioned in Revelation 13:18. Used today as a symbol to identify a satanist or satanic practices.

adept A person skilled in the practice of magick.

Aleister Crowley Called "the wickedest man in the world," he is the man responsible for modern satanism. He died in 1947.

Aiwaz The spirit guide of Aleister Crowley.

amulet An object, not man-made, endowed with a magical power to bring about good or evil.

Anton LaVey Spiritual leader of the Church of Satan. Many of his teachings can be found in Aleister Crowley's works. He has helped pave the way for present-day satanism.

Ascended Masters People (spirits) who have supposedly reached the highest level of spiritual consciousness and have become the guides of the spiritual evolution of the human race.

Ashe The power that resides in the Yoruba gods and the sacrifices that are given to them.

asiento The ceremony in which a person becomes a santero.

astral projection The supposed ability of the soul to transcend one's physical body.

astral world A spirit world from which everything in the material world exists.

astrology A method of divination used to inform a person of the individual course of his or her life, based upon the positions of the planets and zodiacal signs at the moment of their birth.

Azazel The name of a demon that inhabits the desert in Leviticus 16:6-10.

babalawos The high priests of Santeria.

Black Mass A reversal and profaning of the Catholic Mass.

Book of Shadows Also called a grimoire. A journal of spells, traditions, rituals, and thoughts of a person or a group of persons.

cabala   An ancient occult mystical system of interpretation with Jewish roots designed to answer questions about the nature of God, the universe, and the destiny of the human race.

channeling   Supposedly the contacting of a higher life form, the spirit of someone who has died, or an Ascended Master. A modern day term for necromancy.

Church of Satan   Founded by Anton LaVey in 1966.

coven   Traditionally, a group of thirteen witches or satanists that share a common goal. Today it describes a group of witches that work together for a common goal. The number in the coven is thirteen or less.

Dungeons and Dragons (D&D)   A popular fantasy role-playing game.

deliverance prayer   The private action (prayer) of an individual in the name of Jesus. Deliverance prayer is not exorcism. It is a prayer to free someone from demonic oppression.

demonology   The study of demonic spirits.

dissociation   A defense mechanism that is used to defend against pain. When a person dissociates they separate from the memory of a painful event.

divination   The pseudo-science of predicting future events or exploring past events through occult means. Forbidden in Deuteronomy 18:9-11.

ebbo   The herbs and blood of animals used in sacrifices in Santeria.

Eggun   The spirits of one's ancestors.

Eleggua   The orisha who carries the offerings to the other orishas.

elekes   Necklaces given to people involved in Santeria. They are a protection against evil.

Elizabeth Clare Prophet   A popular New Age teacher. Co-founder with her late husband Mark of the New Age cult The Church Universal and Triumphant.

enneagram   A personality theory that uses Sufi numerological divination to assist in self-discovery. This theory states that there are nine personalities in the human race.

exorcism   The Christian ritual for freeing a possessed person from a demonic spirit, which is performed by a priest. In order to perform an exorcism one must have the permission of the bishop of the diocese.

exorcist   Priest who performs an exorcism. Each Catholic diocese is supposed to have an exorcist appointed by the bishop.

FFF   A mark of Satan, similar to 666.

gnosticism   A heresy of the first century. Gnostics believed that a person attained eternal life through secret knowledge.

goathead Symbolizing the horned goat, this is one of the satanist's ways of mocking Christ as the Lamb who died for the sins of humanity.

heresy In the context of this book—a teaching that contradicts the Bible and the teaching of the Catholic church.

Hermes Trismegistus Greek name for the Egyptian God Thoth.

hesychasm An Eastern Christian spirituality from the sixth century that is rooted in the Bible.

horned hand A sign of recognition for those involved in the occult. It is also a sign of the fans of the Texas Longhorns athletic teams.

idolatry The act of worshiping a false god.

ifa A method of divination used in Santeria.

karma The "debt" accumulated against a soul as a result of good or bad actions committed during one's life (or past lives).

limpieza A ceremonial cleansing in Santeria.

Lucifer The name of Satan before the fall. The name means "light bearer."

Lucumi Name given to the Yoruba people in Cuba. This also refers to the language of the Yoruba people.

magick The style of magic practiced by Aleister Crowley. He added the "k" to magic to distinguish his black magick from other magic.

major arcana A set of twenty-two cards used for divination.

medium One who practices necromancy.

MPD Multiple Personality Disorder. The existence within the person of two or more distinct personalities or personality states, each with its own relatively enduring pattern of perceiving, relating to, and thinking about the environment and self. At least two of these personalities or personality states recurrently take full control of the person's behavior.

moyuba The sacrificial prayers of Santeria that are used during a ceremony.

Myers-Briggs A personality test that has been scientifically verified and is used in psychology today. This test states that there are sixteen personalities in the human race.

New Age Movement (NAM) An informal, loosely knit organization that is bound together by common values and a common vision. Some of these ideas are: 1) a coming new age of peace highlighted by human spiritual development, 2) reincarnation and karma, 3) a person's potential is limitless because her or she is divine.

necromancy Attempting to foretell the future or receive knowledge of past events through communication with the dead. This is forbidden in Deuteronomy 18:9-11.

nirvana   Paradise.

Olodumare   The central, creative god of the Yoruba people.

Orishas   African gods of the Yoruba people.

ouija board   A method of divination. The board is made of pressed cardboard. The board contains letters of the alphabet and numbers. A glass platform moves across the board spelling out the answers to questions asked of it.

palmistry   A system of divination through study of the human hand.

pantheism   Religious belief that "all is God." God is everything, everything is God.

peace sign   Originally a sign for peace in the 1960s, occult groups use it today as a sign that represents the defeat of Christianity.

pentagram   Perhaps the most widely used satanic symbol. It is used to conjure up evil spirits.

Pentateuch   The first five books of the Christian Bible.

pinaldo   Ceremony where a santero receives the ceremonial knife for sacrifices.

possession   The state of a person when the devil has such control over the body of an individual that they become, as it were, a blind and docile instrument of Satan's perverse and despotic power.

purgatory   A place of cleansing from the effects of sin in one's life. Judas Maccabeus prays for the dead and asks God to forgive their sins (2 Mc 12:42-46).

reincarnation   The belief that one's soul lives a succession of lives, gradually evolving into a perfect state, usually reached when a person becomes one with the infinite and impersonal God.

rod and pendulum   Similar to the ouija board, it is a system of divination which used a rod with a pendulum attached to spell out the answers to questions asked of it.

Santeria   A religion that has its origins with the Yoruba tribe of Africa. It is a blend of African tribal religion with Roman Catholicism. The Yoruba gods are syncretized with the honor given the Catholic saints.

Santero   A priest of Santeria.

Satan   Proper name for the devil found in Job 1:6-12. He rebelled against God and became the leader of the demonic spirits.

satanic cross An ancient Roman symbol that questions the validity of Christianity.

satanic "s" A thunderbolt that means "destroyer."

satanism Any religious system that incorporates the worship of Satan.

scarab beetle Ancient Egyptian symbol of reincarnation. It is believed to be a source of protection from others within the occult realm.

Silva Mind Control A technique taught by José Silva, in which a person learns how to contact spirit guides.

sorcery (traditional) Attempting to make a pact with Satan to attain power in order to influence events in the world.

soul mates The belief that souls are bisexual in the astral world. When they come to the material world they split into male and female. If these two halves meet each other in the material world a great attachment forms between them and they become conjoined.

spirit guides Demonic spirits or spirits of people who have died and are not at rest with God.

spiritist A person who practices necromancy.

satanic ritual abuse (SRA) Involves forcing a child to do something against his or her will that is repulsive or offensive to the normal sensibilities of decent people. Examples of SRA are forcing a child to eat feces or drink urine, eat an animal's sexual organs, or consume the flesh or blood of a human corpse.

Sufi A sect of the Muslim religion that was involved in mysticism.

talisman A man-made object endowed with a magical power to bring about good or evil.

tarot A pack of seventy-eight cards, containing the twenty-two cards of the major arcana.

Temple of Set One of the public satanic churches, founded by Michael Aquino. He used to be a member of the Church of Satan.

theosophy An occult system of religion and philosophy founded by Helena Blavatsky in the late 1800s.

Transcendental Meditation (TM) A system of meditation made popular by Maharishi Mahesh Yogi in India. It is based upon Hindu religious concepts. It is a religion in itself.

Tree of Life A method of divination of the cabala. The Tree of Life is used to explain how God, human beings, and the earth relate to each other.

Udjat The all-seeing eye refers to Satan, the king of hell.

upside-down cross A mockery and rejection of the cross of Christ.

Wicca A nature religion. Contemporary witches and witchcraft groups follow the Wiccan beliefs.

witchcraft (traditional) Attempting to gain control of the world through curses and spells.

Yoruba An African tribe that lived in present day Nigeria.

Bibliography

Abbott, Walter M., ed. *The Documents of Vatican II*. New York: Corpus Books, 1966.

Ante-Nicene Christian Library. Edinburgh, London: T & T Clark, 1884.

Baer, Randall. *Inside the New Age Nightmare*. Lafayette: Huntington House Inc., 1989.

Balducci, Corrado. *The Devil*. tr. by Jordan Aumann, O.P. New York: Alba House, 1990.

Beesing, Maria, O.P., et al. *The Enneagram*. Denville: Dimension Books Inc., 1984.

Brennan, Joseph. *The Kingdom of Darkness*. Lafayette: Acadian House, 1989.

Buckland, Raymond. *Buckland's Complete Book of Witchcraft*. St. Paul: Llewellyn Publications, 1990.

Chandler, Russell. *Understanding the New Age*. Dallas: Word Publishing, 1988.

Cooper, John. *The Black Mask*. Old Tappan: Fleming H. Revell Company, 1990.

Creme, Benjamin. *The Reappearance of the Christ and the Masters of Wisdom*. London: The Tara Press, 1980.

Crowley, Aleister. *Magick in Theory and Practice*. New York: Dover Publications Inc., 1929.

Cruz, Joan Carroll. *Eucharistic Miracles*. Rockford: Tan Books and Publishers, Inc., 1987.

The Diagnostic and Statistical Manual of Mental Disorders (DSM-III-R). Washington, D.C.: American Psychiatric Association, 1987.

Ensley, Eddie. *Sounds of Wonder*. New York: Paulist Press, 1977.

Faricy, Robert, S.J. *Seeking Jesus in Contemplation and Discernment*. Westminster: Christian Classics, 1987.

The Fathers of the Church. New York: Christian Heritage Inc., 1948.

Friesen, James,Ph.D., *Uncovering the Mystery of MPD*. San Bernardino: Here's Life Publishers, 1991.

Galde, Phyllis. *Crystal Healing*. St. Paul: Lewellyn Publications, 1988.

Gonzalez-Wippler, Mingene. *A Kabbalah for the Modern World.* St. Paul: Llewellyn Publications, 1987.

_____. *Santeria, the Religion.* New York: Harmony Books, 1989.

Gould, Catherine, Ph.D. *Conference on Satanic Ritual Child Abuse.* Malibu: Pepperdine University, 1986.

Gray, Eden. *The Tarot Revealed.* New York: New American Library, 1988.

Groeschel, Benedict. *Spiritual Passages: The Psychology of Spiritual Development.* New York: Crossroad Publishing Company, 1983.

Groothuis, Douglas. *Unmasking the New Age.* Downers Grove: Intervarsity Press, 1986.

Harris, Charles, C.S.C. *Resist the Devil.* South Bend: Greenlawn Press, 1988.

Hunt, Stoker. *Ouija, the Most Dangerous Game.* New York: Harper and Row Publishers, 1985.

Johnston, Jerry. *The Edge of Evil: The Rise of Satanism in North America.* Dallas: Word Publishing Company, 1989.

Keating, Karl. *Catholicism and Fundamentalism.* San Francisco: Ignatius Press, 1988.

Kelsey, Morton. *Discernment: A Study in Ecstasy and Evil.* New York: Paulist Press, 1978.

Koch, Kurt. *Christian Counseling and Occultism.* Grand Rapids: Kregel Publications, 1972.

Kuthumi, Djwal Kul. *The Human Aura.* Livingston: Summit University Press, 1972.

LaVey, Anton. *The Satanic Bible.* New York: Avon Books, 1969.

Larson, Bob. *Satanism: The Seduction of America's Youth.* Nashville: Thomas Nelson Publishers, 1989.

LeBar, James. *Cults, Sects, and the New Age.* Huntington: Our Sunday Visitor Inc., 1989.

Leithart, Peter and Grant, George. *A Christian Response to Dungeons and Dragons.* Fort Worth: Dominion Press, 1987.

Lasalandra, Michael and Merenda, Mark. *Satan's Harvest.* New York: Dell Publishing, 1990.

L' Osservatore Romano. English Language Edition. Rome: Nov. 23, 1972.

Library of Nicene and Post-Nicene Fathers, Second Series. New York: The Christian Literature Company, 1984.

Maloney, George, S.J. *Prayer of the Heart.* South Bend: Ave Maria Press, 1981.

_____. *TM and Christian Meditation.* Pecos: Dove Publications, 1976.

Martin, Walter. *The New Age Cult.* Minneapolis: Bethany House Publishers, 1989.

_____. *The New Cults.* Ventura: Regal Books, 1980.

McAll, Dr. Kenneth. *Healing the Family Tree.* London: Sheldon Press, 1984.

McAlear, Richard. *Deliverance 1988 (conference on deliverance).* Jacksonville: Christian Healing Ministries, 1988.

McKenzie, John, S.J., ed. *Dictionary of the Bible.* Englewood Cliffs: Prentice Hall, 1990.

Metz, Barbara, S.N.D., et al. *The Enneagram and Prayer.* Denville: Dimension Books Inc., 1987.

Miller, Elliot. *A Crash Course on the New Age Movement.* Grand Rapids: Baker Book House, 1989.

Montague, George, S.M. *Our Father, Our Mother: Mary and the Faces of God.* Steubenville: Franciscan University Press, 1990.

Murphy, Joseph M. *Santeria, an African Religion in America.* Boston: Beacon Press, 1988.

The New Catholic Encyclopedia. New York: McGraw Hill Publishers, 1967.

The New Encyclopedia Britannica. Chicago: University of Chicago, 1986.

The New Jerome Biblical Commentary. Englewood: Prentice Hall Publishing, 1990.

Ouseley, S.G.J. *The Power of the Rays.* Romford, Essex, England: L.N. Fowler and Company Ltd., 1951.

Pacwa, Mitch, S.J. *Catholics and the New Age.* Ann Arbor: Servant Publications, 1992.

Palmer, Helen. *The Enneagram.* San Francisco: Harper and Row Publishing Company, 1988.

Peck, M. Scott, M.D. *The Road Less Traveled.* New York: Simon and Schuster, 1978.

Rahner, Karl, ed. *Encyclopedia of Theology: The Concise Sacramentum Mundi.* New York: Crossroad Publishing Company, 1975.

Riso, Don Richard. *Understanding the Enneagram.* Boston: Houghton Mifflin Company, 1990.

The Rites of the Catholic Church. New York: Pueblo Publishing Company, 1976.

The Roman Ritual: Rite of Baptism for Children. New York: Catholic Book Publishing Company, 1970, 1977.

Roman, Sanaya and Parker, Duane. *Opening to Channel.* Tiburon: H. J. Kramer, Inc., 1987.

Scanlan, T.O.R., Michael and Cirner, Randall. *Deliverance from Evil Spirits: A Weapon for Spiritual Warfare.* Ann Arbor: Servant Publications, 1980.

Silva, José. *The Silva Mind Control Method.* New York: Pocket Books, 1977.

Smith, F. LaGard. *Crystal Lies.* Ann Arbor: Servant Publications, 1989.

Spence, Lewis. *An Encyclopedia of Occultism.* Secaucus: The Citadel Press, 1960.

Waite, A. E. *The Holy Kabbalah.* New York: Carol Publishing Group, 1990.

Veritas Catholic Youth Magazine. Los Angeles: Paul Lauer, March/April, 1988.

A Book on Satanism for Parents, Teachers, Pastors, and Youth Workers

When the Devil Dares Your Kids
by Bob and Gretchen Passantino

The occult is a growing threat in America, a danger so real that parents cannot simply assume their children will escape unscathed. If you want to protect your child from the occult, or if you suspect your child is already involved, this book will offer you the spiritual insight, guidance, and practical help you need.

Satanism, witchcraft, and other occult practices lure even "good" kids into a dark world of destruction and pain, a world that can dramatically alter a child's personality, behavior, and important relationships.

Bob and Gretchen Passantino offer expert advice to parents, teachers, pastors, and youth workers. They conduct cult research and are authors of *Witch Hunt* and the award-winning *Answers to the Cultist at Your Door*. Together they direct Answers and Action, a non-profit educational organization, and host a radio program of the same name. They are perhaps best known for their close association and work with the late Dr. Walter Martin, a renowned cult expert. *$8.99*